BUSINESS COMMUNICATIONS IN CANADA

Refining Your Professional Skills

D1400942

BUSINESS COMMUNICATIONS IN CANADA

Refining Your Professional Skills

**Business Communications in Canada:
Refining Your Professional Skills**

Copyright ©2018 DDE Media Company
DDE Media Company
Guelph, ON

Printed in China.
1 2 3 4 11 10 9 8 7
Library and Archives Canada Cataloging in Publication

ISBN 978-0-9940225-5-4

Contributing Writers: Jessica Groom and Adrien Potvin.
Editorial Director: Lyle Shepherd
Proofreaders: Jason Regular, Andrew Webb, Evan Tigchelaar,
John Charles, Sandy Ho, and James Tennant
Content Consultant and Grammar Appendix prepared by Linda Francis
Layout & Design: Cornelia Svela
Cover by Cornelia Svela (with icons from freepik.com)

Contents

Chapter 5 - Developing Oral Communication Skills 117

Chapter 6 - Meetings and Presentations 153

Foreword

Communication is the most powerful tool at your disposal, and nowhere is this more true than in business.

Many business students, especially first language English speakers, do not realize the importance of mastering the skills of business communication. Poor communication skills in business result in inefficient work forces, poor perception and professional image, and lost business and sales. A corporation needs all of these things working well to succeed.

This book is about communication, but you will quickly find that this book is actually an English business communication resource. English is not only the dominant language of North America–the majority of multinational companies have decided on English as their corporate language, which means they conduct the majority of their business communications in English.

However, there is more to business communication than language. There are inherent subtle differences when you compare communication in different countries, even when the language is the same. For example, the Canadian spelling of some words is different from the American spelling (i.e., colour and color, cheque and check, or practise and practice).

This book approaches business communication from a Canadian perspective. Part of being an effective communicator is accepting that your audience may not share your first language. This is a common challenge for communication within Canada, one of the most multicultural countries in the world. Additionally, Canada also has a second national language, French, which a significant portion of the country speaks as their first language.

The aim of this book is to prepare everyone to communicate effectively in a business setting—whether they already have a degree in English, or they are new to business and English is a second language. Starting with the intricacies of language and written English then moving into oral communication, this book will prepare your communication skills for a career in business and teach you to project yourself in a clear, confident, and capable manner.

Developing Written Communication Skills

Welcome to Business Communications! We designed this textbook to send you on your way to communicating professionally, clearly, and courteously through every step of your business career. Whether you communicate through emails, progress reports, marketing sheets, or any other number of communications media, you need to be fluent in grammar, style, and syntax.

Many consider English to be one of the most difficult languages in the world to learn. Even native English speakers break common **grammar** rules on a regular basis.

Though reading often, writing frequently, and developing your vocabulary are the most important ways to improve your grammar skills, it is imperative that you know the basics of grammar, syntax, and sentence structure. They will help you master the language for both business and everyday purposes.

Mastering grammar takes practise. Even people who have been speaking English their whole lives need to practise their grammar skills every now and then. This chapter seeks to help people new to the English language, and native speakers alike, develop their written communication skills.

1.1: The Basics of English Grammar[1]

Constructing Sentences

Before we look at nouns, verbs, and the functions of other kinds of words, let's take a look at what elements comprise a **sentence**. Sentences, next to words themselves, are the most important unit of communication.

A simple sentence has two components: a **subject** and a **predicate**. The subject is the person or thing that acts or is described in the sentence. The predicate is the action or description of the subject in the sentence.

Let's take a look: The car drove down the street.

- What drove down the street? – "the car" (subject)

- What did the car do? – "drove down the street" (the predicate)

The predicate can consist of an adjective, verb, preposition, or any combination of descriptors. In the sentence *She is pretty*, "she" (the girl) is the subject, and "is pretty" is the predicate. The predicate does not need to be just a verb or verb phrase. In this case, the verb "is" and the adjective "pretty" work together to describe the girl.

A group of words called clauses make up sentences. An independent clause is a clause that can make a sentence on its own. A dependent clause is one that cannot be on its own and still make grammatical sense. Take this sentence, for example:

When I was in Mexico, I had a great time.

- "When I was in Mexico."
  (does not make grammatical sense)

- "I had a great time." (makes sense)

"When I was in Mexico" is a dependent clause and does not make sense on its own, but "I had a great time" is an independent clause because it *does* make sense by itself.

When a sentence begins with a dependent clause, it *must* end with an independent clause, like in the above example. Let's look at another one:

When he failed the class, he was upset.

1) *Purdue Online Writing Lab,<https://owl.english. purdue.edu/>*

As you can see, *he was upset* works as an independent clause because it makes sense on its own. The adjective *upset* follows the pronoun *he*. In addition, the verb was (the past tense of the word is) connects the subject and the predicate in the sentence.

If a sentence begins with an independent clause, a dependent clause does not need to follow it. However, if a dependent clause does follow, watch your **comma** usage. While many sentences of this type require a comma, others do not, depending on the conjunction used to connect the clauses.

I ran to the store because we needed milk.

- "I ran to the store" is the independent clause, and "because we needed milk" is the dependent clause.

- In this case, the conjunction *because* links the two clauses. (We will talk about conjunctions in detail later in the chapter!)

Types of Sentences

Now that we have gone over the construction of a sentence, let's look at a few different types.

Simple sentences are sentences with one independent clause and no dependent clause(s).

That dog is cute.

Compound sentences have multiple independent clauses and no dependent clauses. A conjunction connects these clauses.

That dog is cute, and its fur is soft.

Complex sentences have an independent clause and at least one dependent clause.

When I was downtown earlier today, I saw a cute dog.

Compound-complex sentences consist of multiple independent clauses and one or more dependent clauses.

When I was downtown earlier today, I was running errands, and as I crossed the street I saw a cute dog.

Did you know?

Linguistics scholar Noam Chomsky coined a famous sentence in 1957: the sentence says, "Colorless green ideas sleep furiously." While this sentence technically makes no sense, it is also grammatically correct. It is important to distinguish between syntax and semantics!

Definite and Indefinite Articles

In English, there are two articles: definite articles *(the)* and indefinite articles *(an/a)*. Let's look at both.

We use a **definite article** *(the)* before a noun or adjective when the word is specific to something. The subject of the phrase or sentence needs to be a particular thing.

> I will start *the* car.
> We lost *the* football game last night.
> *The* dog is happy.

An **indefinite article** (the word "a" or "an") is used before a *non-specific* noun or adjective. To use "a" or "an" depends on the vowel or consonant sound of the first letter of the noun following the article. There are some tricky rules that you must follow when using indefinite articles, whereas using *the* is more straightforward.

Use the article "a" before words that begin with a consonant sound and "an" before words that begin with a vowel sound.

> It was *a* funny sight.

- Notice how funny begins with "f," a consonant.

> *An* apple fell on Sir Isaac Newton's head.

- The hard sound of the "n" needs to compliment the "a" in "apple."

> It was *a* funny sight when *an* apple fell on Sir Isaac Newton's head.

However, you should be aware that some consonants have different sounds, such as the consonant "h." When you use an article before a noun beginning with "h," use "an" if the "h" is soft, as in hour. Use "a" if the "h" is hard, as in hotel.

> I will book *a* <u>h</u>otel room in *an* <u>h</u>our.

If a word begins with a vowel or vowel sound, the indefinite article will always be "an." Nothing changes depending on if it is a long or short vowel sound.

In English, you may also use indefinite articles to show that something/someone belongs to a group of nouns.

Michael Ondaatje is *a* Canadian author.

- There are many Canadian authors.
- Michael Ondaatje is just one of them.

Jerry is *an* ambulance driver.

- Jerry is just one of many ambulance drivers.

my notes

....
....
....
....
....
....
....
....
....
....
....
....
....
....
....
....

Did you know?
The word "the" is the only definite article in the English language.

Nouns

Now, let's look more in-depth at the kinds of words themselves. We will start with nouns. In short, **nouns** are the names of people, places, or things, and are typically broken up into three different groups:

- **Common nouns**: a common noun is a name for something. It denotes the object as a group or general class of objects or qualities.

  car, ocean, cup, desk, depth, forest
  The *depths* of the *forest* are unreachable by car.

- **Proper nouns**: a proper noun is a specifc name given to something. This can be the name of a specific person, place, or name of a brand or type of object. Always capitalize proper nouns.

  Tom Hanks, Montreal, MacBook
  Tom Hanks lost his *MacBook* in *Montreal*.

- **Compound nouns:** these are **noun phrases** containing more than one noun.

  gas station, hockey rink
  There is a *gas station* next to the *hockey rink*.

It is also important to make the distinction between **concrete nouns** and **abstract nouns**. Concrete nouns are things that can be touched and felt (table, chair, road). Abstract nouns are qualities or ideas (beauty, justice). Abstract nouns are rarely proper nouns.

Identify the concrete noun and abstract noun in this sentence:

The book was given to him with kindness.

- The concrete noun is "book," and the abstract noun is "kindness."
- Since "kindness" cannot be touched and does not really exist in the physical world, it is an abstract noun.

Pronouns

A **pronoun** replaces a noun so we do not have to repeat the noun continuously. There are many types of pronouns, including **subject, object,** and **possessive** pronouns. The noun a pronoun replaces can be either known or unknown.

However, the pronoun must agree with the noun it is replacing. If the noun is masculine, the pronoun must be as well. If the noun is plural, the pronoun must be plural.

Using pronouns can be complicated, so it takes some practice to learn the difference between the different types. This section goes over the different kinds with examples so you can spot them in any sentence.

- **Subject pronoun**: used when the pronoun itself is the subject of the sentence or phrase. Remember—a pronoun works to replace a noun. In this case, the subject (pronoun) performs the action of the verb in a sentence.

  _____ went to the beach.

  - If *went* is the verb (past tense of *go*), who is the *subject*?

  - Could be *I, they, she, he,* etc.

  - You can rename the subject using subject pronouns, if they follow *to be* verbs, which we will address later in the chapter. The *to be* verbs are underlined in the following example.

  It is *I* who is to blame.
  This is *he* speaking.

- **Object pronouns:** used for either direct or indirect objects, or when the noun is not the *subject* of the phrase or sentence.

  I gave it to *him*.
  They took her *wallet*.

  - In the first example, "him" is the object, and in the second, "wallet" is the object.

  - You need to pay attention to the *action* or *description* of the subject to distinguish between subject and object pronouns.

- **Possessive pronouns:** pronouns that show possession of something (*his, hers, theirs, my, mine, yours, ours*).

  That shirt is *mine*.
  This house is *ours*.
  My stomach hurts.

- **Personal pronouns:** these pronouns can come in three forms.

  - First-person (who *is* speaking), second-person (who is being spoken *to*), and third-person (who is being spoken *about*).

  - Here is a chart outlining the different kinds of personal pronouns.

	Subject singular	Subject plural	Object singular	Object plural
First Person	I	We	Me	Us
Second Person	You	You	You	You
Third Person	He/she/it	They	Him/her/it	Them

Some examples:

- *I* missed my train today. (first-person subject singular)

- It doesn't make sense to *us*. (first-person object plural)

- I miss *you*. (second-person subject singular)

- All of *you*, listen up. (second-person subject plural)

- All of *them* are good workers. (third-person object plural)

- *They* are going to walk the dog. (third-person subject plural)

- **Indefinite pronouns:** indefinite pronouns do not need an **antecedent**, as you identify them with either singular or plural general words.

  somebody, nobody, something, anything (Singular)
  Somebody is running down the street.

  all, some, most, both (Plural)
  Most people like going to the park.

- **Reciprocal pronouns:** these pronouns express a relationship or action that both people share.

  Mark and Alice love *each other*.
  Mark and Jason don't like *each other*.

my notes

....
....
....
....
....
....
....
....
....
....
....
....
....
....
....

Verbs

Along with nouns and pronouns, **verbs** are among the most important building blocks of the English language. The verb is the **action** in a sentence, and it connects the noun(s) and pronoun(s) to the rest of the sentence.

There are many types of verbs, including but not limited to, **transitive verbs, intransitive verbs**, and **linking verbs**. Let's look at each of them.

Transitive verbs: these verbs take the *action* of the subject and apply it to the object. It must have a direct object that *receives* the action of the verb.

> She *took* the car for the weekend.
> He *painted* on the canvas.

- Here, *car* and *canvas* are the direct objects in each sentence.

Intransitive verbs: these verbs do *not* affect an object, but express actions that do not require the subject to do another thing. They do not require a direct object.

> He *disappeared*.
> They *left*.
> I was *worried*.

Linking verbs: these verbs explain the link between the subject and the rest of the sentence.

> Jennifer *is* upset about losing the race.

- Most linking verbs are forms of the verb *to be* (e.g., is, are, was)

- The word "is" connects "Jennifer," the subject, to the object "the race."

Some words are both action verbs and linking verbs, like the words prove, smell, and feels. Let's see how they work.

- I *feel* the rough sandpaper. (action verb)
- Jerome *feels* sick today. (linking verb)

Finite verbs are verbs that are the main verb of a sentence.

> He *fought* hard to keep his job.

Non-finite verbs are verbs that cannot be the main verb of a sentence—another verb must modify them. There are three main kinds of non-finite verbs: **gerunds, participles**, and **infinitives**.

Gerunds: gerunds are verbs that function as a noun when an "-ing" suffix is added to the end of the verb (we will discuss suffixes in more detail later in the chapter).

> I enjoy *reading*.
> She went *fishing* yesterday.

Participles: participles are verbs that function as adjectives by adding either an "-ed" or "-ing" suffix to the end of the word. There are **present participles** and **past participles**—present participles usually end in "-ing," and past participles end in "-ed," "-d," "-en," and other suffixes. Let's look at both.

> She put the noodles in the *boiling* water. (present participle)
> After a few minutes, they were *cooked* perfectly. (past participle)

Infinitives: infinitive verbs are verbs with "to" in front of them. There are two parts: the *infinitive* ("to"), and the *base* (the verb itself). The verbs *be, have, sleep, cook,* and *eat* are all infinitive when you place "to" in front of them.

He likes *to cook* for his friends and family.
"To die, to sleep, to sleep, perchance to dream." – a line from William Shakespeare's play Hamlet.
"To strive, to seek, to find and not to yield." – a line from Lord Tennyson's poem "Ulysses."

Adverbs

Adverbs are words that modify a verb, noun, adjective, or another adverb. There are many adverbs in the English language. They often fall into these four categories: *time, place, manner,* and *degree/extent.*

Here are some examples of each:

Time: *now, yesterday, today, daily, soon.*

I'm leaving *now.*
He left *yesterday.*
She is leaving *today.*
The train to Montreal leaves *daily* at 6 a.m.
They will be leaving *soon.*

Place: *here, there, everywhere, nowhere.*

My house is right *here.*
She is over *there.*
There are flies buzzing *everywhere.*
It was *nowhere* to be found.

Manner: *quickly, easily, slowly, beautifully.*

The dog ran *quickly* to the tree.
I passed that test *easily.*
Time moves so *slowly* at work.
She plays the piano *beautifully.*

Degree: *very, mostly, too, enough.*

It was *very* humid today.
He was *mostly* a good student.
Not *too* much sugar, please.
My coffee is hot *enough.*

Hint:
in many ways, adverbs answer the question "how." Adjectives do not do this— they simply modify and describe the noun itself.

Knowing the difference between adjectives and adverbs is crucial, especially when they often occur in the same phrase or sentence. Where adjectives modify the qualities of a noun, adverbs modify the adjective itself.

Let's see how adverbs do this. In these examples, the *adverb* is in *italics* and the <u>adjective</u> is <u>underlined</u>.

I ate a steak last night.

- In this sentence, there is no adjective or adverb. Was the steak any good? Was it bad? Let's see...

I ate a <u>delicious</u> steak last night.

- That's better! Now we know it was delicious. However, how delicious was it?

I ate an *extremely* <u>delicious</u> steak last night.

- Mmm, sounds great! In this sentence, *extremely* is the adverb used to modify how <u>delicious</u> the steak was.

In many ways, adverbs answer the questions "how." Adjectives do not do this—they simply modify and describe the noun attached to it.

How <u>fast</u> did the dog run?—*very* (adverb) **fast** (adjective)

How <u>well</u> did the pianist play?—*beautifully*

my notes

....
....
....
....
....
....
....
....
....
....

Tenses

Tenses are extremely important when making a sentence. The **tense** of a verb expresses the time when the action took place.

There are three core tenses of verbs: **past, present, and future.** However, within those three groups, there are a handful of subcategories, making for twelve main tenses in total.

Let's look at them in chart form. Pay attention to how the *be* verb works with the tenses.

	Past	Present	Future
Simple	I *ran* down the street to take the bus.	I *run* down the street to take the bus.	I *will run* down the street to take the bus.
Continuous	I *was running* down the street to take the bus.	I *am running* down the street to take the bus.	I *will be running* down the street to take the bus.
Perfect	I *had run* down the street to take the bus.	I *have run* down the street to take the bus.	I *will have run* down the street to take the bus.
Perfect continuous	I *had been running* down the street to take the bus.	I *have been running* down the street to take the bus.	I *will have been running* down the street to take the bus.

my notes

Subject-Verb Agreement

The order of the subject, object, and verbs define all languages. How these words work together depends on how you arrange them. English is an SVO (subject-verb-object) language, which means you must follow this order when constructing sentences.

Mark (*subject*) kicked *(verb)* the ball *(object)*.

The major rule of subject-verb agreement is that you need to pay attention to the number of the subject and verb. If a subject is singular, then the verb must also be singular. Let's take a look.

For these examples, the subject will be <u>underlined</u>, and the verb will be in italics.

The <u>river</u> *flows* fast.
The <u>rivers</u> *flow* fast.

As you see here, when the subject is singular, an "-s" or "-es" suffix must be added to the verb. There is no suffix on the verb when the subject is plural.

Another important rule is that a phrase or clause in between the subject and verb does not change the number of the subject. Remember, the verb must agree with the number of the subject that the verb modifies, not other subjects or nouns in a sentence.

Incorrect: The <u>steaks</u> left on the counter *was* rotten.
Correct: The <u>steaks</u> left on the counter *were* rotten.

A collective noun is another class of noun, referring to a group of individuals. When the subject you are modifying is a collective noun, pay close attention to the verb, as collective nouns can appear as singular or plural.

Incorrect: The <u>class</u> *laugh* at the teacher's jokes.
Correct: The <u>class</u> *laughs* at the teacher's jokes.

Incorrect: The <u>people</u> *laughs* at the comedian's jokes.
Correct: The <u>people</u> *laugh* at the comedian's jokes.

Adjectives

Adjectives are words or phrases that describe or modify a noun, or the noun's qualities. The adjective usually comes before the noun, but not in every case. An adjective can come in the form of a single word, phrase, or clause.

In these sentences, the noun is <u>underlined</u> and the adjective is in *italics*.

> Janelle wore a *pretty, flowery* <u>dress.</u>
> It was a *dark* and *stormy* <u>night.</u>

Sometimes you will use an adjective after the noun, called a **postpositive adjective**, but this is often for artistic or poetic purposes in English. It is a largely out-dated way of speaking, which is why you often find it in poetic language and others reserve it for titles of artistic works.

> John Milton's long poem *Paradise Lost.*
> The jazz album *A Love Supreme* by John Coltrane.

However, some words still use the postpositive adjective, like in the phrases "time immemorial," "accounts payable," and "poet laureate."

Adjectives can also come in the form of **adjective phrases,** which are groups of words in which the adjective is the main word. A modifier may accompany the adjective.

> Houston, Texas is the *fastest-growing* city in the United States.
> The mountain range was *extraordinarily beautiful.*

my notes

....
....
....
....
....
....
....
....

Conjunctions

Conjunctions are words that join clauses and phrases together. There are three types of conjunctions: **coordinating, subordinating**, and **correlative conjunctions.**

Coordinating conjunctions are conjunctions that join two independent clauses into the same sentence. Words that are coordinating conjunctions are "but," "and," "yet," and "or," among many others. In these examples, the conjunction is in italics.

Without coordinating conjunction:

> I want to go swimming. Paul wants to play golf.

With conjunction(s):

> I want to go swimming, *but* Paul wants to play golf.
> I want to go swimming, *yet* Paul wants to play golf.

Subordinating conjunctions are conjunctions that introduce subordinate or independent clauses. Some examples are the words and phrases "after," "although," "now that," "since," "when," and "until."

> The car is broken, *although* I got it fixed last week.
> He hasn't seen her much *since* she was busy with her new job.

Correlative conjunctions are pairs of conjunctions that connect two subjects and/or clauses. These kinds of conjunctions link two words or clauses that are grammatically similar. Therefore, a noun must connect to a noun, an adjective must connect to an adjective, et cetera.

Here are some pairs of correlative conjunctions:

> *As* far *as* I know, she will be coming late to dinner.
> *Not* tonight, *but* tomorrow night.
> *Not only* is he a bad worker, *but also* a rude person.
> *Neither* Joel, *nor* his friends, caught their bus.

With correlative conjunctions, there needs to be a pronoun-antecedent agreement. Let's look at that last sentence above. Notice how the pronoun is "their," because it is not only Joel who missed his bus, but his friends as well.

Prepositions

Prepositions are words that indicate location or time. There are many different prepositions, so we will separate examples into two lists: one for time, and one for location.

Even for native English speakers, prepositions can be difficult as there are few rules on using them. They usually follow a noun, but this is not always the case. These are not complete lists, by any means, so feel free to search for other examples of prepositions!

Location/Position/Direction

Preposition	Usage	Example
On	- something attached - on a surface - for a floor	The mirror *on* the car... ...*on* the table ...*on* the 13th floor
At	- events - a place with a specific purpose - for the word table	*at* the park *at* the movies (cinema) eat your dinner *at* the table
In	- a room, street, country - picture - a book	*In* Canada... ...*in* the office ...*in* that picture *In* Herman Melville's book Moby-Dick...
Below	- underneath something	We stood *below* the overhang to avoid the rain.
From	- in a different location	I took this shovel *from* the shed.
To	- movement to somewhere/something	They are going *to* the beach
Across	- getting to the other side of something	The farm is *across* the river and *across* the plain.

Time

Preposition	Usage	Example
At	- a certain point in time - for evening/day/night	We will eat dinner *at* 9 p.m. The racoons come out *at* night.
Ago	- a time in the past	That was ten years *ago.*
Since	- from a certain time in the past (until the present)	Serving you proudly *since* 1959.
On	- days of the week	We shall meet *on* Monday.
For	- over a certain period of time (until the present)	"We have been in business *for* over 30 years."
Until/till	- marking the beginning and end of a length of time; how long something will last	I work from Monday *until* Friday. There will be no deliveries *until* next week.
Before	- earlier than a specific point	He never called me *before* yesterday.

my notes

....

....

....

....

....

....

Other Prepositions

Preposition	Usage	Example
From	- who gave something	You have a message from Isaiah.
Of	- who/what something belongs to	Open to page 256 of your textbook.
By	- who made something	She bought a purse by Gucci.
About	- topic	We talked about the hockey game.
Off	- leaving public transit	He got off the bus.
At	- for someone's age	He moved to Vancouver at 22 years old.

my notes

....

....

....

....

....

....

....

....

....

....

Prefixes and Suffixes

Prefixes and **suffixes** are sets of letters used at the beginnings (prefix) and endings (suffix) of words to give them a new meaning, or, in the case of suffixes, change what kind of word it is (a verb can become an adjective, etc.).

Common prefixes:

Prefix	Meaning	Example
un-	- not	unsatisfied, unappealing, unworthy
in-, im-, ir-	- not	injustice, impossible, irregular
super-	- above something (either physically, qualitatively, or otherwise)	superlative, supernova, supermarket
anti-	- against something	antibacterial, anti-climactic
semi-	- half of something	semi-detached, semi-finals
de-	- opposite	defrost, debone
hyper-	- beyond/more than normal	hyperactive, hypertension

Common suffixes:

Suffix	Meaning	Example
- able	- something that can be done or had	comfortable
- ed	-past tense of a verb	jumped, ripped
- ous, - eous, - ious	- having a quality	nauseous (has nausea) Joyous (has joy)
- less	- without something	homeless, graceless
- en	- made of	flaxen, wooden
- ism	- a doctrine or belief	catholicism, capitalism
- ment	- a process	movement, government

These are only some of the most common examples, meaning that these lists are not all-inclusive. Now that you have learned how to spot prefixes and suffixes, try looking for them in every day words and see how they change the meaning of the word!

my notes

....
....
....
....
....
....
....
....
....
....

Spelling: Tips and Hints

Though there is usually a spell check feature on the software we type with (Microsoft Word, Google Docs), it is still important to know how to spell well without the aid of a spell checker.

These spell checkers cannot catch everything, and they usually do not account for grammar and/or syntax. As a result, you will need to rely on an understanding of spelling rules when it comes to spelling properly—especially if a word is spelled correctly but may be contextually incorrect (to, too, two; sew, so; their, they're, there).

Good spelling is just as important as good grammar. Since there are so many words in the English language that are spelled similarly, words that sound the same but mean different things, and differences in spelling based on region (Canadian spelling is sometimes different than American), it can be overwhelming to spell some words properly.

Here's a handy trick that should help with commonly misspelled words: draft a list of words you often misspell in one column on a sheet of paper, and in the next column, write the correct spelling. Use this website to help you with common grammar issues: **http://grammar.yourdictionary.com/spelling-and-word-lists/misspelled.html**

It could look a bit like this:

Misspelling	Correct spelling
Recieve, decieve, percieve	Receive, deceive, perceive
Alottment, comittment	Allotment, commitment
Acommodate	Accommodate
Definetely	Definitely
Maintnance	Maintenance
Occurance	Occurrence
Perserverence	Perseverance

1.2: Punctuation

By this point, you should be familiar with the basics of English grammar. We will now move to **punctuation**, which provides us visual cues for how a sentence should flow, what the tone is, what is possessed or pluralized, et cetera.

The following are the most basic punctuation marks you will use.

Apostrophes

The **apostrophe** (') has many uses: it can be used in a contraction (*do not = don't, cannot = can't, should not = shouldn't*), or to put words into a possessive case (the *boy's* lunchbox, the *girl's* skateboard).

Periods

In English, we use a **period** (.), or "full stop", to indicate the end of a sentence.

Commas

The comma (,) is a difficult punctuation mark to master, along with the semi-colon. Using commas separates clauses and groups of words into an order. Let's look at some proper uses of commas.

Rule #1: Commas separate nouns into lists.

> Tetsuo brought a backpack, a tent, some food and water, and clothes to the music festival.

Rule #2: You should use the **Oxford comma** unless a style guide says otherwise. The Oxford comma is inserted before the "and" in a list, you should have a comma to separate that "and" from modifying the word before it.

> My heroes are my parents, Superman and Wonder Woman.

- They're not your parents! … are they?

> My heroes are my parents, Superman, and Wonder Woman.

- If they aren't, then this is the correct use for the comma.

The comma is also important to indicate the logic of a sentence. Example:

> Let's eat Grandpa!
> Let's eat, Grandpa!

Colons and Semicolons[2]

The **colon** (:) and **semicolon** (;) are used for listing nouns and adjectives. The function of the colon as opposed to a comma for lists is that everything after the colon must compliment or modify what came before it.

> There are only three things I don't like: spiders, avocados, and improper colon use.

The **semicolon**, on the other hand, is one of the most misused punctuation marks in the English language, if not the most misused. Let's look at some rules for the semicolon.

1. We use semicolons to link two independent clauses that are closely related in thought.

> Some people like tomatoes on their sandwich; others prefer pickles.

2. Use a semicolon if either a conjunctive adverb or transitional phrase connects two independent clauses.

> While Toronto is a big city, it is not too difficult to navigate the TTC subway; there is an easy-to-read map in each station.

3. Avoid using a semicolon to connect a dependent and independent clause if there is a coordinating conjunction.

> This would be wrong:
> Though I should have been; I was not upset.

2) Writer's Handbook, University of Wisconsin – Madison. Retrieved July 9, 2015.

Italics

Indicating titles of things and adding emphasis are two uses for italics. In most citation styles, such as MLA (the Modern Language Association) and Chicago Styles, the titles of books, journals, publications, and films and TV shows are italicized.

When citing, use "quotations" for essays, journal articles, scientific/technical reports, poems, and short stories rather than italics. Always be sure you know which style guide you are following when writing a text. Also ensure that your citation and reference style is always consistent.

- Titles:

  I went to see the film *Whiplash* last night.
  The New Yorker is my favourite magazine.
  James Joyce wrote the famous book *Ulysses*.

- Emphasis:

  I *told* you not to do that.
  We *could* eat Chinese food, but I'd prefer Italian food.

- Foreign languages:

  The only thing I could think was, "*c'est la vie*."
  (C'est la vie: "that's life")

Quotation Marks

Quotation marks (" ") are used for recording speech, and quoting written material that is not your own. Let's see how both work in their respective purposes.

- For speech:

  "Will you please quiet down?" asked the teacher.

- For quoting someone:

  At the Brandenburg Gate in 1987, Ronald Reagan famously said, "Mr. Gorbachev, tear down this wall."

Commas and periods should always go inside quotation marks. If the quoted phrase ends in a question mark, do not capitalize the first word outside of the punctuation.

Question Marks and Exclamation Marks

Use a **question mark** (?) for an interrogative sentence, or to ask a question. Interrogative sentences always have an **interrogative pronoun** such as "who," "what," "when," "where," "why," and "how."

> Where do you want to go for lunch?
> How much wine should I buy?
> Why did you do that?

An **exclamation mark** (!) indicates emphasis. Think of it this way: an exclamation mark has the same effect as when you raise your voice when you speak.

> I didn't know that!
> That guy almost hit me with his bike!
> What an incredible view!

my notes

....
....
....
....
....
....
....
....
....
....
....
....
....
....
....

1.3: Advanced

Now that we have gone over the basics of English grammar, and you're well on your way to practising your grammar and writing skills, let's go over some more advanced skills you should work on.

Again, practise makes perfect. You need to read and write often in order to master the English language. Grammar can only take you so far—you'll also need to understand tone, point-of-view, and diction.

Active vs. Passive Voice

For most purposes, the expectation is that you will write in the **active voice.** The active voice is difficult to spot at times (especially when you are the one writing), but it is nonetheless important to be aware of this voice.

The active voice is preferred in most writing for three reasons: it makes your writing more concise, the text flows better, and it places the reader directly into the action.

Let's go over how to spot the active voice and how to write in it.

In active voice, the subject is the one completing the action and comes first in the sentence.

I *walked* to the store. "I" is the subject.

In **passive voice**, the target of the action takes the place of the subject in the sentence.

The store was *walked* to by me. The subject in this sentence should be "me," but the target (the store) is taking the subject's place.

Passive voice isn't incorrect but it does make sentences longer and more difficult to understand. Passive voice can be useful when the subject is unknown or intentionally obscured.

Mistakes were made. The subject that made the mistakes is unknown, so this phrase is passive.

Protip:
In Microsoft Word, under File > Options > Proofing, you can set your grammar checker to underline where you are using the passive voice.

Which one of these sentences is in the active voice? Hint: there is only one.

Dinner will be cooked for us tomorrow night.
I drove miles to get here.
The book was taken from the shelf.

Answer: the second one.

1.4: Writing Styles –
Technical, Professional, Conversational

Whatever you are writing, you will need to make sure you know the appropriate style for your writing. Different situations call for different tones of voice and levels of diction, so it is important to make sure that you know the audience to whom you are writing before you begin the research stage.

There are many different writing styles. For the purpose of this textbook, we will focus on the kinds of writing you will be doing the most for business purposes: technical, professional, and conversational.

We will elaborate on all of these further on in this book. For now, here is a general overview of what these writing styles need.

Technical Writing

Technical writing takes on many forms. Technical writing is about explaining more than entertaining, and technical writers write about various topics from computers to machine instructions and medicine.

The key to good technical writing is being brief and to the point. Consider this example: you are writing a manual for assembling a bed. Will the reader want to waste time on reading unimportant details about what the wood grain on the bedframe looks like? Your writing might be descriptive, but it is not relevant. Chances are your reader just wants to build their new bed so they can get a good night's sleep.

Keep irrelevant details out of your technical writing. Stay on topic and maintain a logical flow throughout every step. Since technical writing is often concerned with actually performing the described actions—such as constructing a bed or programming a computer—ensure your writing is clear, logical, and easy to understand.

Conversational Writing

Conversational writing is writing in a tone of voice and level of language meant to open up a conversation. Good conversational writing relies on a less formal level of language, as well as good "people skills." You will want to put your own personal touch into any conversational writing you do.

You will usually use conversational writing in emails, blog posts, and other electronic communications. You may even use it for marketing. Some press releases and white sheets are quite conversational and personal.

Argumentative Writing

Argumentative writing is a style of writing that makes an argument and supports it, both logically and in terms of tone. The kinds of argumentative writing you will see are in critical essays, legal defences, and any other type of writing that tries to state a claim or argument.

When doing an argumentative piece of writing, keep in mind that you should address the opposing view of the argument in question and refute it to strengthen your own stance on the topic.

For example, if you were writing a paper arguing against the use of genetically modified organisms in farming, you could bring up the opposing view that GMOs can make it easier for under-developed countries to access seeds to grow crops. Your refutation could come along the line that selling the seeds isn't a sustainable economic practice and that over-reliance on seeds from Western corporations does not help the countries' development.

1.5: The Writing Process –
Writing, Editing, and Proofreading

The writing process can be a daunting one, however following these seven steps will help you organize your thoughts, write properly, and determine the appropriate level for your audience. We will look at these topics more in-depth in the fourth chapter of this book, but a brief overview of the writing process now will help.

Knowing Your Purpose

Before you begin writing a piece, you need to know the purpose of your writing. Writing styles have various purposes: *fiction* aims to entertain; technical writing aims to explain things; argumentative writing seeks to argue and defend a theory, idea, or opinion; and persuasive writing sells products and services and establishes brand loyalty, among other marketing-related practises.

Knowing your purpose (KYP) before starting to write will help you at every step of the writing and revision process. Before beginning each project, ask yourself a few key questions:

- What point of view do I hold with this piece?
- What is the audience to do at the end of my communication? Do something? Know something? Be better informed? Be able to do something?
- If it is an argumentative piece, how do you plan to argue your stance?
- If your writing is for people within a particular field, what level of language do you need to use?

Making your purpose clear from the outset will help you organize your thoughts, get to a clear resolution at the end of your work, and keep the whole writing process generally more organized.

Knowing Your Audience

After you have established a purpose for your writing, you now need to consider whom you are writing for—Know Your Audience (KYA).

- Is your audience composed of native English speakers, or English as a Second Language speakers?
- Are they in the field or profession you are writing for?
- What level of education does your audience have?
- What are their hot buttons on this issue (if any)?
- Are they friendly or hostile?
- What do they already know about you/your topic?

When considering your audience, think about diction. Diction is the way you use words and phrasing. Let's look at some good and poor diction.

Use technical **jargon**—complex words and concepts used by a particular profession—sparingly. If your audience is unfamiliar with terms specific to one job or field, your point will be lost in difficult wording and you will leave your audience confused. If you are going to use jargon, you need to define the terms. If you think your audience will be unfamiliar with these terms, it is best to leave them out of your writing.

If you are explaining a concept understood by those in your profession, but not others, use language that is simple but still describes the concept in full. Proper diction is one of the greatest challenges you will face as a writer.

"I made mistakes in drama. I thought drama was when actors cried. But drama is when the audience cries."

- Frank Capra, director of It's a Wonderful Life

Brainstorming

Before creating an outline, do some brainstorming. Using your purpose and audience, think about the logical flow your writing will follow. Use whatever brainstorming method works for you. A common technique is "spider" or "cloud." Write the topic in the center of a piece of paper, draw a circle around it, and then draw lines extending from the circle and put down as many ideas as you can think of without editing them. Just get everything out on the page. Idea generation is the goal here; edit later.

You may also need to do some research at this point.

You can ask yourself questions like: who would be interested in this? Why do I, or others, care? How would things be different if this didn't exist/happen? What is my least/most favourite aspect of this issue? How would someone react to this?

Once your brainstorming is done, eliminate the ideas you don't think directly relate to your topic.

Prioritize the remaining topics.

Outlining

After you have brainstormed some key ideas about your topic, your next step is to create an outline for those ideas. Making a good outline is not only about putting the ideas onto paper, but also making a logical flow for the direction of the text to take.

Take the points you've brainstormed that are the most closely related. Arrange them into a list based on the priority you gave them in the brainstorming session. Leave room for notes and more points so you can flesh out each section of your piece. Put points under each idea and ask yourself questions, such as:

- What is this?
- Why does it relate to my main idea?
- How is it impacting my communication?
- What could happen if something else happens?
- What else could happen because of it?

"My only writing ritual is to shave my head bald between writing the first and second drafts of a book. If I can throw away all my hair, then I have the freedom to trash any part of the book on the next rewrite."

- Chuck Palahniuk, author of Fight Club and Choke.

First Draft

At this point, you should be just about ready to work on a first draft! A first draft is simply a rough edition of the text you are writing. Don't worry, it will not be perfect: it is a starting point.

A first draft should contain your core ideas. When you revise your work, you need to delete as well as add concepts, double-check sources, re-write entire paragraphs, and make many other changes. This is normal, so don't get caught up on every single word or sentence you choose in a first draft.

Take your outline and write from it. Expand upon the points in the outline, creating full sentences and paragraphs.

No first draft is perfect—mistakes are inevitable.

Editing

After you have brainstormed, researched, outlined, and written your first draft, the editing process can begin. Editing is the most time-consuming and important part of your writing process. This is where you'll make the major changes to your draft. Your ideas and paragraph and sentence structure may change drastically during this stage.

At this stage, add specific, relatable examples and details where necessary. You can check transitions and word choices, double check figures and data, and expand upon ideas.

Proofreading

The proofreading stage is where you make changes to grammar, punctuation, and spelling. Do not confuse the proofreading and editing stages—in proofreading, you are focusing on your mechanics. You should do this yourself and get at least one other person to proofread your piece. Also, consider printing your material on paper so that it is easier to read and mark up with a red pen or highlighter.

Regardless of the purpose for your writing, always make sure to follow these steps. Whether it is a report, email, or blog post, going through these stages at least twice is crucial to ensuring your communications are accurate and readable.

Chapter 1 Quiz

1) Identify the noun in the following sentence: The car was red.

    a. The
    b. Car
    c. Red

2) Identify the adverb in the following sentence: I like when Jessica plays the piano, she plays so beautifully.

    a. Jessica
    b. Plays
    c. When
    d. Beautifully

3) What can a prefix do to a verb?

    a. Make the verb an adverb
    b. Make the verb a conjunction
    c. Make the verb an adjective
    d. Make the verb a noun

4) Which of the following sentences is NOT in the passive voice?

    a. Mary cooked dinner for her friends.
    b. The ball was thrown by James.
    c. After a night out, I was driven home by my father.
    d. The glass of milk was knocked over by the cat.

5) What is a gerund?

6) What type style is used mainly for emphasis and to cite titles?

    a. Question mark
    b. Italics
    c. Quotation marks
    d. Infinitive

7) An apostrophe, when placed after a noun and before an "S," does what to the noun?

    a. Makes the noun an independent clause
    b. Makes the noun an adjective
    c. Makes the noun possessive
    d. Makes the noun a participle

8) Identify the tense in the following sentence: My family will be eating dinner at 6:30 pm.

    a. Future continuous
    b. Present perfect
    c. Future imperfect
    d. Present continuous

9) What part of the writing process should you spend the most time on?

    a. Writing
    b. Editing
    c. Proofreading
    d. Production

10) What does a sentence need to be grammatically correct?

    a. Participle and subject
    b. Subject and adverb
    c. Compound and predicate
    d. Subject and predicate

Answers:

1. (B) 2. (D) 3. (C) 4. (A) 5. (A noun made from a verb by adding an "-ing" suffix – ex: running, cleaning) 6. (B) 7. (C) 8. (A) 9. (B) 10. (D)

Reading

Being able to read fluently and effectively affects everything we do and is an asset for anyone. We need to read words, signs, numbers, and countless other things every single day.

Frequently, reading can be a challenging task, especially with difficult material like charts, case studies, and expense reports. It requires your eyes, mind, and body to work in sync to both recognize and understand words, signs, and concepts. These are all core parts of **reading comprehension.**

Reading efficiently for business requires considerable practise, patience, and a dedication to learning. We need to read many items, such as business reports, emails, transportation schedules, and progress reports. When working in a business environment, it is critical to ensure that everyone communicates clearly and effectively.

Knowing how to read these items fluently will ensure that everything runs smoothly for yourself, your colleagues, your clients, and your employer. Always remember—communication, clarity, and comprehension are key.
This chapter outlines some ways in which we can improve our reading skills and reading comprehension.

Learning Goals

By the end of this chapter, you should be able to:

1. Read more quickly and efficiently after working on some useful reading comprehension exercises and techniques.

2. Use speed reading to increase both your reading speed and comprehension.

3. Use muscle reading to use your body in getting the most out of your reading comprehension.

4. Read digital material (Google searches, databases, emails, reports) more effectively.

5. Ask in-depth questions and interpret facts through critical reading.

These skills are necessary in a business setting in which we are required to work through far more information in a faster paced environment than ever before.

Reading is pleasurable, relaxing, and can teach you much more about understanding language than simply knowing how it works.

2.1: Developing Reading Skills

Reading quickly and efficiently requires practise and dedication. There are a number of ways to practise your reading and reading comprehension skills at home, on your way to work, and at work, which will keep your skills honed. You need to practise the skills we cover in this chapter constantly to stay at your peak.

- **Skimming**: quickly reading over something to understand the core idea

- **Scanning:** reading quickly, but looking for specific information

- **Intensive reading:** reading with attention to detail and with a specific task in mind

- **Extensive reading**: reading for pleasure to improve your skills and understanding of the language

You may need to use these techniques at any point, even when you might not expect to, so it helps to train often. It is easy to trick yourself into thinking your reading is improving if you are not aware of exactly *how* it is improving. Stay aware of what aspect you are working on!

Skimming

Skimming means reading over something quickly to understand the main idea behind it. While doing this may not give you a deep understanding of the material, you will understand the main points conveyed in the text.

For example, perhaps you are reading the newspaper on the city bus. However, before you finish the article you are reading, the bus arrives at your stop. Although you didn't finish the article before you stepped off the bus, you still understand the core idea of the article.

By skimming through the text you are reading, you train your eyes to receive information quickly, and your eyes find the most important information.

Use the *"who, what, where, when, why, and how"* principles when skimming. Practising this works especially well with newspapers, because newspapers are written to keep information focused, brief, and easy to read. The main ideas are usually contained within the first paragraph of an article's body.

Skimming Challenge: The next time you pick up a newspaper, go to any article and try to answer the "Five Ws and an H" as quickly as you can. The idea is to scan the article quickly, while also capturing the main points. You will have to do this often, as this skill will take some practise to perfect.

Skimming Challenge Exercise

Using the sample email, assume that you need to answer this email quickly. You need to be able to skim through large blocks of text to get the key points. From one quick read, identify:

- Which restaurant Colin wants to meet at for lunch
- At what time?
- How late Denise will be for lunch.
- What do you plan for the three of you to discuss?

Hi Joe,

Glad to hear your report turned out so well. I heard it went over great and that Frank was really happy with it.

Are we still on for lunch today? I was thinking we'd meet up at that place at Bloor and Spadina we went to last month—I think it was Jimmy's Deli—at, say, 1pm? Their smoked meat sandwich is out of this world, and it's pretty affordable. Oh, also, I'm not sure if you saw that email or not, but Herman told us to go easy on the expense accounts. So, maybe no surf and turf for a week or two, eh?

Denise is going to join, but she said she would be about half an hour late. Is that okay? I figured it would be, and we can just have a drink before she gets there. I don't know about you, but I could use one after that staff meeting, am I right? They said it'd only be fifteen minutes and it took an hour and a half! They really need to plan those better, I tell you.

I thought we'd go over the last little bit of the Penske file, so we can stay on top of it. It's been at a good pace so far, but since it's due in a few weeks, I think we should keep up the pace and maybe work a bit more on it. No pressure, though. I just have lots to do this week, so I'd like to get this out of the way as soon as we can if possible. Let me know what you think.

Best regards,
Colin

Since the email rambles, the reader needs to get to the main points. Skimming here allows the reader to determine the major points to put in their day planner. Using skimming, the day planner entry might look like this:

- Meet Colin at Jimmy's Deli @ 1pm
- Denise will be half an hour late
- Look over Penske file

The reader extracted the key information out of the email, even though the body of the email was a bit rambling. Skimming through material to get the gist of it is an effective tactic that you'll use daily in a business setting.

There are many times you'll need to skim through documents for important information.

Scanning

When you read by **scanning**, your eyes are able to pick specific information out of a large amount of text. When you scan a block of text correctly, you can both understand the core idea of what you are reading and pick out the more specific information that you will need. It works in the same way as skimming (to understand the basic idea), as well as digging for more specific information.

An example of scanning is reading and *understanding* train and bus schedules. If you live in an urban centre with trains and buses (which may also connect to other city systems), you do not need to know where every single train or bus in the city goes: you need to know where your train goes. When you search a train schedule to find out what time it arrives or leaves, you are *scanning* already!

Scanning is perhaps the most important reading technique you can practise. Determining schedules, whether it is commuting schedules or juggling meetings at work (which may also require commuting), are common tasks in the business world.

You can extend this reading technique to other tasks at work—reviewing status reports, emails, expense reports, articles in professional journals, budgets, and so on. You'll also apply it to day-to-day tasks such as reading flyers, buying groceries, and evaluating and locating contractors and/or other services.

How many times have you been overwhelmed by a plane or bus schedule? Learning to scan properly can be of great help.

Intensive Reading

Intensive reading is perhaps the most important technique to use when interpreting data and information. An educational example of intensive reading would be a *close reading* exercise in a literature class. The instructor assigns a short passage from a novel, short story, or poem. They then expect the students to read into what the text *means,* by way of its word choice, metaphors, style, et cetera. In business, you may do this to interpret a sheet of data, a business proposal, a technical report, or an expense report.

Learning the mechanics of the language is important to communicating well. Furthering your understanding of how language works is very important, so that you can use language in any setting. Not everything you read will be written and primed for reading comprehension exercises, but you should still practise intensive reading often.

Extensive Reading

Extensive reading, or reading for pleasure, is the opposite of intensive reading (focused on detail-oriented reading).

Intensive and extensive reading can be compared to the two parts of a driving test: *intensive reading* is the part of the test you write in the classroom, and *extensive reading* is the road test. The biggest difference between the two is that intensive reading focuses on reading to learn and extensive reading focuses on learning to read.

The benefits of extensive reading for business communications include:

- Improved vocabulary
- Improved writing skills
- Language problem solving (ability to see wording, tone, details, et cetera)
- Interpersonal communication skills (understanding humour, tone)
- The joy of reading

There will be times in your business career where you'll find yourself overwhelmed with emails, reports, and deadlines. Pleasure reading during your spare time can be a wonderful escape from the bustle of the workweek. It can offer a sanctuary for you, improve your diction, sharpen your mind, and make you more creative.

Being creative is what gets people hired and promoted, and something that earns the respect of your colleagues and bosses. It is worth your while to read extensively and truly enjoy the craft of reading and writing.

2.2: Speed Reading

Comprehending reading and *practising* reading are quite different, though the two do work hand-in-hand. **Speed reading** is a technique you can use to train yourself to read quicker. However, don't forget that you need to actually *understand* what you are reading. Practising your speed and comprehension are equally important.

Picture yourself working in a position where you are required to review reports, respond to emails, attend meetings which require you to address the agenda topics, and review technical journal information and/or financial data from sites related to your job. You are required to review and manage this daily input of information in your job. Speed reading is the crucial skill you need to stay on top of the daily flow of information.

The average person can read approximately 200 words per minute (wpm), but with speed reading you can go up to 500 wpm. How *useful* speed reading is has been in debate since its emergence in the 1950s and 1960s, but there is no doubt that it helps your reading skills in big ways.

There are three major aspects of speed reading with which you should familiarize yourself:

- Subvocalization
- Chunking
- Using a pen/finger/index card

Subvocalization

The largest hurdle you will face when practicing speed reading is **subvocalization**. You can probably hear it now just reading this—subvocalizing is that very faint voice at the back of your head, reading aloud along with you. It can also involve silently moving your mouth to read words to yourself.

Subvocalization is not necessarily a bad habit. That little voice in the back of our minds helps our vocabulary, increases our reading comprehension, and helps us read more efficiently overall. Nevertheless, when we need to read something quickly, it becomes more of a burden and an impediment to reading as quickly as we can.

Fun fact:
Former U.S. president John F. Kennedy was a practitioner of speed reading and encouraged his staff to do the same!

We were taught from a young age to read words aloud or in our heads, which makes this a difficult habit to break when it comes to speed reading. Here are some tips to help silence the subvocalizing voice:

Do something with your mouth: Chew on a piece of gum, a pen, or anything else to keep your mouth from moving along with your reading.

- Keeping your mouth busy will prevent you from mouthing each word as you read along, and help to silence the subvocalizing voice in the back of your head.

Listen to instrumental music: Ambient or instrumental music will help drown out that voice in the back of your head.

- This allows it to become less intrusive so you can focus on reading and comprehending much quicker.

- Classical music has been found to be the best for this.

Cover what you have read, or guide yourself: Though it is frowned upon by some, it generally helps to quickly track where you have read with a pen, your finger, or covering the page with an index card or bookmark.

Exercising speed reading can be fun and useful, but remember that comprehension and retention are quite important as well!

Did you know?

Howard Berg was featured in the 1990 Guinness Book of World Records as the world's fastest speed reader —he allegedly read 25,000 words in one minute!

Chunking

Spend less time reading every word you come across in a paragraph, page, or sentence, and instead place them into one chunk of text. This technique will help your reading speed in a big way.

Chunking involves both placing words together to read them quicker and removing the words that slow you down. You should be able to understand something even though you have eliminated actively reading the *a, an, to, it, et cetera,* from a passage. Focusing on these words takes up little time, but it adds up when you are trying to read faster.

This also works for whole sentences, lines of text, and even entire pages. By grouping individuals words into one visual plane and cutting out subvocalization and distractions, you are on your way to increasing your reading speed.

Chunking also involves orienting your eyes to take in as much visual information as it can. This can take on the form of reading diagonally and in other directions.

Our eyes naturally flow from the start of one line to the next, but we can train ourselves using our peripheral vision (what we can see at the corners of our eyes) to cross our eyes across the pages we read and take in more information from the text as a whole.

Buyer Beware – Apps and Websites

Ever since speed reading first became a popular practise in offices and schools, many individuals and companies have tried to sell us the next best program, promising increased reading speed and comprehension.

Save yourself the trouble and don't buy into these. More often than not, they do not work. You can achieve the same, if not better results by working on speed reading using the guidelines listed above.

Scanning/Chunking Practise

Below is a paragraph from Mark Twain's classic book *The Adventures of Huckleberry Finn*. The passage is 336 words. How fast can you read the passage using what you have learned about speed-reading techniques?

1. Time yourself reading the passage with a stopwatch or timer.
2. Use this formula to determine how many words you can read per minute.
   - Words per minute (WPM) = (number of words in passage ÷ reading time (in seconds)) x 60
3. Answer the comprehension questions at the end of the passage.

"Now the way that the book winds up is this: Tom and me found the money that the robbers hid in the cave, and it made us rich. We got six thousand dollars apiece—all gold. It was an awful sight of money when it was piled up. Well, Judge Thatcher he took it and put it out at interest, and it fetched us a dollar a day apiece all the year round—more than a body could tell what to do with. The Widow Douglas she took me for her son, and allowed she would sivilize me; but it was rough living in the house all the time, considering how dismal regular and decent the widow was in all her ways; and so when I couldn't stand it no longer I lit out. I got into my old rags and my sugar-hogshead again, and was free and satisfied. But Tom Sawyer he hunted me up and said he was going to start a band of robbers, and I might join if I would go back to the widow and be respectable. So I went back.

The widow she cried over me, and called me a poor lost lamb, and she called me a lot of other names, too, but she never meant no harm by it. She put me in them new clothes again, and I couldn't do nothing but sweat and sweat, and feel all cramped up. Well, then, the old thing commenced again. The widow rung a bell for supper, and you had to come to time. When you got to the table you couldn't go right to eating, but you had to wait for the widow to tuck down her head and grumble a little over the victuals, though there warn't really anything the matter with them, — that is, nothing only everything was cooked by itself. In a barrel of odds and ends it is different; things get mixed up, and the juice kind of swaps around, and the things go better."

1. How much of the money did Huck Finn receive?

  a. $6000
  b. $8000
  c. $4000

2. How much did Huck Finn make from Judge Thatcher's interest on the money?

  a. Two dollars a day
  b. Fifty cents a day
  c. One dollar a day

3. The Widow called Huck Finn a "poor lost _____"

  a. Cat
  b. Lamb
  c. Horse

Answers:

1) a 2) c 3) b

How did you do? If you achieved 2/3 or more correct, good work! If you achieved less than 2/3, you need to work on your reading comprehension. Remember, it doesn't matter how quickly you can read if you don't retain it! Keep practising and keep trying to increase both your WPM and retention skills.

my notes

....
....
....
....
....
....
....
....
....
....

2.3: Muscle Reading[3]

Sometimes, it is not enough to only use your eyes and your brain to read—sometimes you must make use of your whole body, and actively balancing as well as focusing your body and brain helps you to read effectively and accurately. That is why practising **muscle reading** makes a difference.

Muscle reading is the weightlifting of reading comprehension techniques. It is an intensive nine-step process, including lots of practise and a keen feel for how the steps and concepts work with each other.

However, those who excel at muscle reading retain more information and have a better grasp of concepts and ideas. For very difficult and long documents, use these tips to get the most out of what you are reading.

For example—if you ever feel yourself overwhelmed with the sheer volume of a case study, report, or analysis you are reading, it helps to simply underline or highlight chunks of text that you find important. You can then refer back to these markings, instead of scanning through the entire document again to find the information.

Before you read	While you read	After you read
Preview	Reflect	Recite
Outline	Underline	Review
Question	Answer	Review again

These nine steps to muscle reading are not necessarily required all in one process, but all of of them should help you concentrate and retain information more efficiently.

Before you start reading, make sure your posture is correct for muscle reading. Make sure you are upright in an office chair, not in bed (comfortable though it may be), and not in front of the television or with other distractions around you, and with a calm mind and clear headspace.

These steps may seem overwhelming, but you do not need to follow them exactly. However, each step does help to strengthen your attentive reading and comprehension skills in some way. Let's take a look at these steps a bit more in-depth.

3) Dave Ellis, "Muscle Reading—Becoming a Master Student," University of Colorado Denver. http://www.ucdenver.edu/academics/colleges/CLAS/clas-advising/Documents/Vlb.pdf

Before You Read *(pry out questions)*

Preparing yourself before reading can help you gain an overview of the text and provide a context for the information and details presented in the text. This preparation is valuable later when you are studying the text and making notes.

1. Preview: Preview the whole thing you are reading.

- For a book, flip through the table of contents or chapter list.
- For a few chapters or an article, leaf through the pages and glance at them. Look for key words, phrases, and chapter headings to get a better grasp of the topic.
- **Summaries** also help a lot in previewing. They often contain the core information from the whole text, helping you obtain a general understanding of the text.

2. Outline: Understand the structure of what you are reading by outlining, either in your head or on paper, what you are going to read.

- Use headings to guide yourself through the logic of what you are reading.
- You should use outlines to build upon as you read further. Sometimes it helps to write one out on a separate piece of paper.
- The outline does not need complete details right away—you will detail it throughout the reading process.

3. Question: Ask yourself what you want from an assignment, and compose questions that seek to answer it.

- Use key sentences or headings and turn them into questions. This helps when it comes to finding questions to ask yourself.
- Compose questions to ask yourself and keep in mind throughout the whole of the reading process. This helps you stay engaged while reading.
- Ask more specific questions as you read to strengthen how engaged your brain is with the material.

While You Read *(root up answers)*

Now that you have started actually reading the text, it is time to fully engage with it.

4. Reflect: Before you begin reading, reflect on what you already know about the subject. This will prime your brain for retaining the information in your long-term memory.

- Break up your reading into short intervals of time or page length, especially if it is a longer or more difficult text you are reading. It is all about setting reasonable goals!
- Here are some techniques you may want to try:
  i. Visualize the material: Form mental pictures and visual imagery of the material you are reading.
  ii. Read the material aloud.
  iii. Get a feel for the subject: This is easier for some topics than others, but still try to use your mind and body to visualize and materialize what you are reading.
  iv. Remember the questions you asked yourself when you started reading, and examine the accuracy of the answers.

5. Underline: Mark your pages with highlighters or pens to keep track of core phrases and concepts.

- Marking your texts helps you retain information better by building a stronger neural pathway in your brain—literally "muscle memory."
- These highlights, ticks, and underlines also make it easier to find information when you go back to review the text.
- Only mark around 10% to 20% of any given text, because if you mark it too much, those markings may become redundant.

6. Answer: Begin answering the questions you asked yourself as you become more familiar with the text you are reading.

- Check these questions and answers with a classmate, co-worker, supervisor, or instructor to see how the question and answer process went and determine the accuracy of your findings.
- Asking yourself questions and finding the answers to them will help you retain information and keep your reading comprehension sharp.

After You Read *(recite, review, and review again)*

After you have finished reading, recite and review your notes and material. It is easy to trick yourself into thinking you are reading with intent. Work on these three steps to ensure that you have retained the information from your reading it. It doesn't matter how much you have read. What matters is how well you retain the info after the fact.

7. Recite: Reciting and paraphrasing what you have read, to yourself or to another person, helps you retain the information you have just digested. It also shows how much you comprehended.

- The most important thing you can gain from reciting the information is summarization.
- Whether you recite it aloud to yourself or someone else, your ability to summarize will affect how well you retain the information you have just learned.

8. Review: Within 24 hours of reading, go back and review the text you have read to retain the more detailed parts.

- This process helps shift information from your short-term memory to long-term memory.

9. Review again: Over the next few days or weeks, review your notes, highlighted and underlined texts, and your outline.

- This review continues shifting the information you have retained from short-term to long-term memory.
- Reviewing over a longer period will keep the information fresh in your short-term memory as well

Everybody has different comfort levels with reading and retention. Find the method that works best for you, and try different ones when you get more comfortable.

2.4: Digital Literacy

Nowadays, we spend more and more time in front of computer screens. Our laptops, desktops, and cellphone screens are almost always in use, especially in a business communications setting. Technology, such as Amazon's Kindle reader, has even changed the way we read for pleasure. These technologies are constantly changing.

How do we keep up with these changes and get comfortable with fluency on computers? With every software update we get on our computers, it seems like there's one new feature after another. Though this can get overwhelming, ask yourself a few important questions:

- How will this help me get the most out of my computer?
- How useful is this feature, and what am I using it for?
- What can this tool or feature do that I can't do without it?
- How will I use this in my workflow? Will it slow it down or make it quicker?

Streamlining your computer experience will help your productivity and overall comfort level with computers in important ways. Being fluent in digital literacy will help not only your reading comprehension skills, but will have you feeling more comfortable with your computer, smartphone, and any other technologies you may use in the workplace.

Digital reading involves practising a few key tactics:

- Making use of reading helpers, like thesauri, dictionaries, and reference tools.
- Knowing how to get the best out of your Google search and other information databases.
- Keeping your computer and cell phone organized and de-cluttered.
- Knowing the difference between reputable and questionable sources/websites.
- Knowing how to read spreadsheets accurately and effectively.

Reading Helpers—dictionary, thesaurus, and reference

Ever find yourself coming across a word you don't quite understand? Or does your writing need a bit more flavour to it?

There are countless dictionaries and thesauri—as websites, apps, and books—you can use to find definitions and synonyms for words.

Mac computers come equipped with a dictionary and thesaurus in the applications folder in the Finder. This software also comes with a reference function that could be useful to get a general gist of something.

Microsoft Word also comes equipped with dictionary, thesaurus, reference, and translation functions. You can find them in the "Tools" menu in the menu bar.

Google Tips—conversion of units, translation, and more

Google is one of the most powerful tools the Internet has to offer. It provides you with all the information you need at your fingertips. However, it can be difficult to navigate sometimes. Google has a number of tools to make your searching experience more intuitive and helpful. Some examples are:

- **Dictionary and thesaurus**: By simply entering a word into the search bar, you can get a definition of it. You can further this by using the thesaurus function as well.

  - Use the DEFINE: function to streamline the definition—there will be the definition and an etymology (history) of the word. This also works for abbreviations and acronyms.
  - To find the definition of RBI (runs batted in—a baseball term), enter "DEFINE: RBI" into the search bar.

- **Unit conversions:** If you need to convert a measurement or currency, simply enter it into the search bar and let Google do the math.

  - 200 centimetres into feet
  - $1000 US to Euros

- **Search websites for keywords**: Suppose you saw something mentioned on a website, but you didn't save the URL or remember what the article was called. Try the formula [keyword] site:[website URL] to find out when the keyword was mentioned on that website.

  - To see how many times the author Ernest Hemingway was mentioned in the magazine *The Paris Review*, you would enter "Hemingway site:theparisreview.org."

- **Use quotes to search for an exact phrase:** Using quotation marks limits your search to the exact phrase.

  - "Now is the winter of our discontent" (Shakespeare, *Richard III*)

If you don't remember the whole quote, you can also use an asterisk (*) to find a variable phrase. What was it again? The winter, or summer, of our discontent? Let's find out.

  - "Now is the * of our discontent"

The Internet is perhaps the most important tool you will use when working in business. You will need to use email, research, social media, and countless other things, so it is important to be fluent and comfortable with computers.

De-cluttering Your Computer—streamlining your work space

As with your own office or living space, keep your computer clean and de-cluttered so you can find information, documents, and other material quickly. However, in the heat of a major project or a particularly busy week, this isn't always possible. Clutter can build up and overwhelm you before you know it.

Folders, backups, and widgets can help you keep your computer desktop and hard drive more organized, de-cluttered, and easier to navigate. Google Drive and Dropbox are great tools for both backing up files and keeping them neatly arranged in folders. If you use a Mac computer, place folders in the dock at the bottom of your screen, allowing for quick and easy pop-up access.

There is no right or wrong way to label your folders and files, but a good tip is to use some kind of slug format. A slug is a readable, brief, and unique format for naming files. Publishers use the slug format to indicate exactly what the file is about in three to four words formatted simply.

The format varies, but generally you want to keep every word in the slug capitalized with no spaces between the words. When you are looking through your files, this will be more visually appealing and easier to read.

Let's see how it looks.

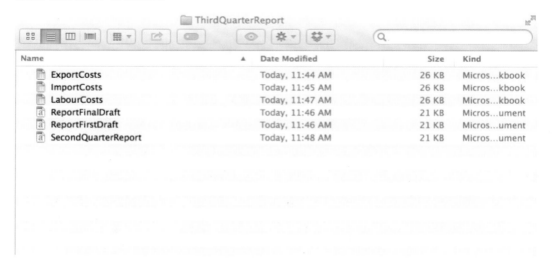

As you can see, the uniform arrangement of file names with all capitals and no spaces is much easier to look at than if each file name was different. Small organizational changes can really help speed up your workflow and streamline your computer workspace.

Sources and Websites—what to look for when researching

If you are doing research on a topic, look for reputable sources of information. This can be tricky on the Internet because of the sheer volume of websites and databases for you to use. However, a few guidelines should help you avoid the website you thought was a bit unreliable. Your guideline for unreliable sites: *If it seems like it is, it probably is.*

- **Check for the publication date**: Does your topic have a use for research published and conducted 50 years ago?

  - Make sure you check the date stamp and date of index (DOI) on sources to ensure they are as relevant as possible.
  - Depending on the discipline or topic you are working with, we suggest you find articles published within the last 10 to 20 years.

- **Look up the publisher or company**: Where the research was conducted can be very important as to deciding if the research is accurate and reputable, with no visible bias or conflict of interest.

  - If you were doing a report on GMOs, for example, which reference would you trust for accuracy—an academic paper published at a respected university, or a press release from a company producing GMO seeds? Things like this can make or break the integrity and transparency of your research.

- **Look up the author:** Is this author well published and well respected in their field? If this is somebody's only publication on the subject, and you have found someone who has done it for their whole career, who would you trust more?

- **Examine the secondary sources:** Chances are, if a report, essay, or analysis is not well supported with secondary sources, then it is not worth using. The author could be presenting their opinions rather than facts.

  - This also goes for using Wikipedia: Since Wikipedia is user-sourced content, it could be skewed or inaccurate. Footnotes are useful in determining where the author got their information. You can find the references at the bottom of the article's page.

2.5: Reading Critically

Another important aspect of reading well is **critical reading**, the definition of which sometimes differs. However, critical reading at its heart means reading a text and interpreting its facts, paying attention to possible ambiguities or logical flaws by the author, and establishing your own opinion on the text in question. You will encounter this kind of reading especially in legal writing and case studies.

Critical reading is particularly important when reading legal reports, analyzing academic papers, and reading various forms of journalism. You should always ask if there is a possible bias in an article, report, or essay.

Essentially, critical reading means that you need to take everything as an argument, with *claims* and *supports* that need to hold up before you accept the text's argument as true. When reading critically, it is best to consider everything you read as an *argument,* no matter how technical the writing is or how well the data is presented.

As we discussed when looking at digital reading, the first step to reading critically is to check the facts when reading an analysis of a topic, a case study, or even the newspaper.

For example, perhaps you are reading a report on the Alberta tar sands and you notice some bias in the presentation of the research. After digging a little deeper, you find that the author has ties with Canadian environmental awareness groups. Does this undermine the article's integrity? This is a *conflict of interest,* and is one of the many things a critical reader must bear in mind.

Chapter 2 Recap

This chapter presented the following concepts:

- Reading comprehension involves a blend of reading fluently and an ability to retain information.

- Scanning and skimming are two practical ways to extract information quickly from large blocks of text.

- Intensive reading has a strict focus on grammar, syntax, and other technical understanding of language.

- Extensive reading is an approach to reading that focuses on reading for pleasure and learning to appreciate the subtleties of language, meaning, et cetera.

- Speed reading is practised to increase reading speed by chunking words, lines and sentences together, as well as eliminating the sub-vocalization and mouthing of words—practises that can impede your reading speed.

- Muscle reading is a more intense process of nine steps that improves your reading comprehension skills, especially when reading a particularly difficult report, essay, or case study.

- Improving your digital literacy skills can help you search easier, interpret spreadsheets more efficiently, de-clutter your workplace, and offers numerous other benefits.

Overall, everyone needs to be able to read well, and everyone should read often. Your company's success as well as your own depends on consistent, concise, and effective communication in every sense.

Chapter 2 Quiz

1) Skimming can be best described as:

a) Reading through material quickly to find a specific piece of information

b) An intensive, nine step process to increase reading comprehension

c) Reading through material quickly to understand the general point of the text you're reading

d) A process in which we read by getting rid of subvocalization

2) Which reading comprehension technique would you use mostly for pleasure reading?

a) Speed reading

b) Intensive reading

c) Digital reading

d) Extensive reading

3) While you are muscle reading, what step ensures that you visualize the material?

a) 4: Reflect

b) 6: Answer

c) 2: Outline

d) 7: Recite

4) What technique would you use when looking at a train schedule?

a) Intensive reading

b) Muscle reading

c) Scanning

d) Critical reading

5) How much of your text should you underline or mark up, ideally?

a) 10%-20%

b) 5%

c) 25%

d) No text

6) Roughly how many words per minute can the average person read?

    a) 200 wpm
    b) 300 wpm
    c) 150 wpm
    d) 500 wpm

7) What would a "close reading" in an English literature class be considered?

    a) Digital reading
    b) Extensive reading
    c) Intensive reading
    d) Skimming

8) Subvocalization is…

    a) The voice in your head that reads along with you
    b) A bad reading habit
    c) Mouthing words to yourself
    d) Humming to yourself while you read
    e) Both A and C

9) True or false—every step in muscle reading is mandatory to doing it properly.

10) You have heard about a new prescription drug that many report causes birth defects. However, you find a new report that strongly denies all these claims. Upon your own further analysis, you find that an independent journalist with ties to a major pharmaceutical company published the article. What is this an example of?

    a) Critical reading
    b) Conflict of interest
    c) An unreliable source
    d) All of the above

Answers:

1. (C) 2. (D) 3. (A) 4. (C) 5. (A) 6. (A) 7. (C) 8. (E) 9. (False) 10. (D)

my notes

Chapter 3

Digital Written Communication

As previously discussed, effective written communications is essential in a business setting. Fluency in the use of emails, IMs, text messages, and other forms is crucial to keeping a steady workflow.

Email is a business tool used to keep co-workers, customers, and suppliers in communication. This chapter will look in-depth at how to write these communications appropriately.

Business communications—whether digital or traditional—include a human element. One common pitfall in business emails is that the intentions and tones (especially tones) behind messages can get confused and misinterpreted. This can lead to tension between the sender and a client or colleague.

This is why it is important to be clear, courteous, and concise when communicating via email. When communicating in writing, bear in mind these potential pitfalls:

- What is the diction like? Are you being too formal, or not formal enough?
    - Overly formal and "wordy" emails can be interpreted as standoffish, pretentious, or condescending.
    - However, if an email is not formal enough, you may sound flippant, unprofessional, or rude.
    - Think of the golden rule: treat others the way you'd like to be treated. How would you like others to address and speak to you? Alternatively, recall the platinum rule: treat others how they would want to be treated (because not everyone will want to be treated the way you would).

- To whom are you writing?
    - If you are writing to a client or a potential client, you will want to be courteous but to-the-point. Don't waste anyone's time, and don't make them feel like they are wasting yours by reaching out.
    - Depending on the colleague, you may be able to get away with language that is more informal in written communications (if they are a friend outside work). However, always err on the side of caution—you never know how somebody can interpret something. We lose all the non-verbal communication tools in email and other non-electronic media: facial expressions, **body language**, and tone of voice.

- What do you aim to accomplish in your communications?
    - If you are trying to sell a product or service to a potential client, it is crucial that you respect their intelligence and answer any questions or problems they may have in a respectful manner. Anticipate any potential hot button issues, challenges, and disputable points, and have answers ready for these if they should arise.
    - If you are dealing with a conflict with a colleague or superior, for instance, your aim will be to work out a plan to fix the problem at the root of the conflict. In doing this, you need to be calm, collected, and act with everyone's best wishes in mind, within reason. If a conflict is being resolved, keep the written communications to a minimum. Schedule a meeting and use an email to recap your discussion(s).

Grammar, tone, and context are three key things to be aware of when it comes to written communication for business. If you are unprofessional in your written communications, it reflects on both you and your employer. Not establishing a proper tone, or sounding rude, could cost you some opportunities. *People remember rudeness as much as they do courtesy, if not more.*

These are just some examples of things to look out for in proper business communications. By the end of this chapter, you should be able to:

- Know the appropriate levels of diction, style, and grammar in which to write emails, text messages, et cetera.
- Know the difference between inter-office and intra-office communications.
- Know how to write for both inter-office and intra-office communications.
- Understand the importance of courtesy and personality when communicating with clients and colleagues in writing and in person.
- Understand how blogging can make you and your company stand out.
- Realize the importance of social media and networking (especially LinkedIn) for you and your career.

Learning Goals

There are always different contexts in which we need to decide on which level of diction and tone is best to use. As mentioned, if something is too formal it could sound pretentious or condescending. However, if it is too informal it can show a lack of care, respect, or seriousness. This is why we always need to be aware of how we are writing something, why we are writing it, and to whom we are writing.

When communicating in business, you always need to be sure of to whom you are writing, why you are writing them, and what both or all parties seek to gain from contacting one another.

3.1: Emailing & Memos

You will likely use email as the main medium of communication between your colleagues, superiors, and clients. Email has become the standard method of business communications in the past two decades because of its speed and ease of use.

Email is an invaluable tool for business, but you must always remember that it has its own set code of conduct and professionalism that you must follow. Emailing colleagues, superiors, and clients is far different from emailing friends and family—this is a business communication tool and you should treat it as such.

Paying close attention to these conventions will make communications clearer and more concise, and will establish you as a reputable, reliable, and professional employee. Mutual courtesy and respect build good business relationships, so reflecting these values in your emails will be important.

However, before we get into those matters of tone and context, it helps to look at the basics of formatting your email first.

Format: The Basics

It is easy to just fire off an email. Anyone can do it. However, it is important to know how to format emails properly for business purposes. The following elements make up a good email:

- a context-appropriate subject line,
- a person and context-specific salutation,
- a text body that is clearly worded, to the point, and about one subject only,
- and a polite and courteous closing line.

Learning what to say, and how to say it, will prove to be invaluable in your business career. For now, let's focus on the nitty-gritty parts of how to format emails.

The Subject Line

Your **subject line** is one of the most important things to understand. A good subject line is informative, but also concise. A good length to aim for is about 40 to 60 characters. This length allows you to strike a balance and fit in enough information to adequately inform the reader about the email's contents, but leave enough out to ensure they open the message.

The purpose of the subject line is to clearly indicate what the email is about. Here are some examples of what to include and when:

- **When applying for a job:** "Application for [position] as referred by [name of reference]."

    - This makes the intent clear and includes a name for receiver to check.

- **When following up an interview**: "[your name] following up on [position]."

    - This also drives the point home of what the position is, and who it concerns (you).

- **When scheduling a meeting**: "Can we meet about the new strategy this Thursday at 2 p.m.?"

    - Having a set date and time prevents your email from coming across as vague and highlights the urgency of the meeting.

- **When issuing a work-related request:** "Reminder: Project Z first draft due August 1" or, "Please return survey form for August 1."

  - If you are reminding colleagues of an upcoming project's due date or other project-related things, chances are good they know about the project's particulars, so you don't need to go into more depth in your subject line.

As you can see, each example listed here is concise enough to address the exact purpose of the email, but long enough to avoid being vague or confusing. A good subject line needs to be relevant, quick, and easy to read, otherwise you run the risk of having your message lost in communication, if read at all by the recipient.

The Greeting and Closing Lines

Similar to how the first words and actions of a conversation set the tone for a conversation, the **salutation** that opens your email is crucial to how your email will be received and perceived by the reader. Unless you are carrying on an already established correspondence, the first lines you will write in your email act as your greeting. Remember that your non-verbal cues are eliminated here (tone of voice, body language, eye contact.) Your message relies on your word choice and diction to set the tone.

Like most factors of written communications, how you choose to start your email depends on context. You need to know, to the best of your ability, who you are addressing and why you are writing to them.

Your greeting can take on many forms, depending, once again, on who you are addressing. Let's go over some common salutations, when to use them, and when to avoid them.[4]

- **"Dear"**: Many people avoid using "Dear" as a salutation because it seems trite, but in reality, it is one of the better salutations to use. If you know the gender of the person you are addressing, preface Ms., Mrs., or Mr. after typing "Dear."

- **"Dear Sir or Madam"** or **"To whom it may concern"**: There is not much use for these out-dated, vague greetings. These kinds of salutations indicate that you did not research whom you are addressing. The former may be read as sexist if the intended recipient does not identify as that gender.

- **"Greetings/Greetings all"**: This works well for addressing a group of people, as it is not too familiar or unfamiliar. You can address people you know well and those you don't know so well using this greeting.

4) Angela Ogunjimi, "Good Salutations for Business Emails," The Houston Chronicle, retrieved June 30, 2015.

- **A simple "Hi [first name]"**: This is good for people you closely work with, but if you are emailing someone for the first time, be wary of using it.

Closers are usually less specific and more courteous. Your choice in closing your letter is largely up to you, as long as it follows more or less the same level of courtesy and address as your salutation does. Some common ones include:

- Best/kindest/warmest regards,
- Talk soon,
- Respectfully yours,
- Thank you,
- Best wishes,

Being appropriate in your addressing and courteous in your choice of closing words is very important. As you can see, an appropriate salutation highlights both the content of the email and makes it clear whom it is addressing.

The Body
The body of the email is where your writing skills will really shine through. A good email has an appropriate length and the body itself should be concise and focused on one subject. Emails about more than one subject are difficult to navigate and will confuse the reader about what the most important subject is.

Sentence length is also important for writing a successful business email. A good rule of any email should be no more than one screen in length. Use proper punctuation, grammar, spelling, and capitalization. When you transition between pieces within an idea, break each piece into its own paragraph.

If your email runs more than one screen, copy the content of the body into a Word document and attach it to the email. Provide a brief introduction to the attachment in the body of the email.

An alternative is to split the email into separate emails, each of which focuses on one piece of the message. Bear in mind that many business people today use their tablets and smartphones to manage their emails.

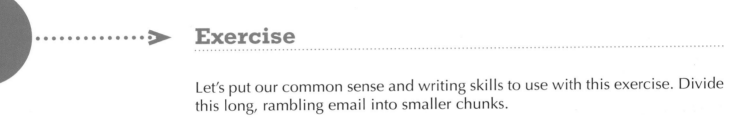

Exercise

Let's put our common sense and writing skills to use with this exercise. Divide this long, rambling email into smaller chunks.

Subject: Market report for 2015
From: Paul Jenkins

Hi Jen,

I'm just checking in about that copy of the report I sent a few days back. How did you find it? I was thinking of cutting out, if not completely then partially, the segment about the New York headquarter report since they got it already a few weeks ago. What do you think? Also, there's a segment in there that I'm not quite sure how to word, and since you're the expert on grammar and content, what should I do? I think it's under section 5.7, where I went over the web analytics report of Q2 of 2014. I'm not sure exactly—I highlighted it, but I don't remember exactly where it is in the report. Anyways, let me know what you think and I'll make the changes as soon as I can and get it back to Jerry.

Thanks and best regards,
Paul

my notes

....
....
....
....
....
....
....
....
....

Take a few minutes to think about how Paul could have re-worded or short-ened his sentences. It should look something like this:

Subject: Edits to market report for 2015
From: Paul Jenkins

Hi Jen,

I wanted to get in touch about that report I sent you the other day. Let me know if you think I should remove the section on the NYC headquarters report, since they already have it from last week.

Also, I could use some help with the wording in section 5.7. I believe it is that one, but I highlighted the section for you to find.

Thanks and best regards,
Paul

Sentence breaks make your point stronger by cutting out filler. They are also easier to read and glance over than a very large block of text. Notice how much easier it is to read your revised example than the first example.

Tone, Style, and Grammar

Just because email is fast and easy to use does not mean you should overlook the importance of grammar, style, and tone. It is easy to slip into this habit. Picture yourself returning from your lunch break to a bunch of emails from colleagues, clients, and vendors. Your first tendency will be to reply as quickly as possible.

Although it is a good thing to be punctual and productive, it is very easy to overlook exactly how you are replying, especially in the heat of the moment, when your email inbox is filling up quickly and deadlines are approaching.

A messy, disjointed email filled with many typos and syntax errors, or an email that sounds passive-aggressive or rude will cost you a lot of time and effort in repairing this miscommunication. Take time at the beginning to craft the right message first.

Subject: Possible demo for batteries?

Hello,

I'm writing on behalf of TelComm Phones, Inc. I hope you're having a great day.

We are a start-up company based out of Newark, NJ, and we were interested in meeting to discuss a contract for the batteries you manufacture. Would you please direct me to whom I would speak about meeting up and doing a demo?

We look forward to seeing what your products have to offer.

Thanks and best regards,
WW

Here are two possible replies to this email.

Reply #1

Hi,

She's out of town for the week. I'll ask somebody who knows.

AP

Reply #2

Hello,

Unfortunately, the person in charge of scheduling demonstrations is away on business, but her contact info is attached below should you like to contact her.

Please don't hesitate to reach out if you have any other questions or concerns.

Best wishes, AP

How would you feel after receiving a reply like Reply #1? It comes off as harsh and cold, doesn't it? Reply #2 is informative, courteous, and concise, where Reply #1 is vague, too brief, and rude in tone. Perhaps AP felt rushed when sending his email, but with his lack of attention to the tone of his reply, he could very well have lost his employer a significant contract.

Having shorter, more informal (but tone-appropriate) emails may be alright with coworkers if it is regarding a quick update or a minor issue being addressed, but you should still remember to be considerate in your wording.

Remember—grammar, tone, and style are the most important things to keep in mind when sending emails!

Inter-office vs. Intra-office

Just as you speak to your professors differently than you do to your close friends, you need to use different levels of language when you communicate with office colleagues, or potential clients/vendors/collaborators.

A good way to determine the level of diction to use is to consider whether the email being sent is inter-office or intra-office. "Inter" means matters with other offices, while "intra" means matters within the office in which you work.

Chances are if you have an email correspondence with someone outside of your office, you will attempt to establish or maintain some kind of business relationship with them. Similarly, your email correspondence with your colleagues and superiors will ensure that everyone is on the same page and that the business is running smoothly.

There are always different contexts in which to communicate with others. Being aware of your purpose for reaching out and of the person's position within a company or office are just a few things about which you need to be conscious.

Inter-office tone/formality

- Be courteous, helpful, and professional.
- If a client needs direction to another department or person, offer them that department or person's contact information and any other details (for example, if they are away from the office).
- If you are making a deal, proposal, or sale of some kind, be sure to respect the person's intelligence and integrity. Do not be dishonest or misleading.
- Don't be too formal. Coming off as overly formal appears condescending, pretentious, or wordy, though you may not intend it.
  - Try to keep a balance between kindness and light-heartedness as well as formal professionalism.
  - Being personable, but professional and formal, will help a great deal in establishing or maintaining a strong business relationship.

Intra-office tone/formality

- There is a bit more flexibility with language when sending emails between colleagues than when connecting with those outside of your office. With coworkers, you can use company jargon, a joke or two (if it's work-appropriate), and a more relaxed tone of voice.
  - Despite this, you must remain professional and courteous. Nobody wants to work with someone who goofs around at work all the time.
  - An occasional joke is usually alright (depending on the joke and the context), but nobody will take you seriously if you are joking around all the time.

- Stay on point: When you are sending emails among colleagues, make the email about one thing and one thing only. As we've gone over, quick-to-read emails are the best.
- Be aware of your organizational structure. An email to a co-worker (or peer) can be more informal/conversational, whereas an email to a manager or vice president should be more formal.

Think of it this way: your written communications with coworkers and clients should reflect some sort of "heightened" version of you. You should have some of your personality in your tone, but it must also reflect a professional manner.

Communicating with Clients and Colleagues

Your clients are your most valuable assets. They are the people with whom you will want to establish a solid business rapport. You will establish a good rapport if there is a mutual respect, appreciation, and consistency in communication between both parties.

However, there are certain hurdles you will face when working with clients, such as cultural differences, conflicts of opinion, and clients and colleagues who do not hold up their end of the bargain.

This section will outline some common issues you will face from time to time with clients, and how to work through these issues together in a courteous, professional manner.

Conflict Resolution

Most people wish everything would go smoothly all the time, and that we could all agree. However, this is obviously not the case. You are bound to have disagreements with clients from time to time. This can span from heated to civil, and from major to minor problems.

All disputes should be resolved with respect, dignity, and everybody's interests in mind (within reason). Good **conflict resolution** skills are a key part of any successful office workflow and positive office culture.

The best way to work out conflicts is in person, but this is not always possible. One party may be working from another city, country, et cetera, so you may need to use email or speak over the phone to work through the problem.

The best way to discuss conflict is person-to-person or voice-to-voice. You can then use email to summarize your conversation to ensure both parties come away with the same results.

Here are some items to keep in mind when resolving an internal or external conflict. You may follow these steps for face-to-face or digital communications. For the purpose of this chapter, we will focus on written communications.

Accountability: In any situation of dispute, one or more parties must be held accountable. This is less an "admission of guilt" or blaming somebody, and more of a practical look at how the situation has unfolded, who was responsible for what, and how the dispute could have been prevented.

- Focus on the issue/problem, not the person. What happened and why? How will it be fixed (if it can)? How is the solution to be implemented? How can this be avoided in the future? If this conflict can help to prevent a future problem, then it has a positive result. Treat the conflict as a learning opportunity for everyone.
- Think of the problem as a whole. You don't want to place the blame solely on one person or part of the situation. It is important not to single people out, so that everyone can agree on a solution.
- Again, your tone is important. Be fair but firm in resolving an issue.

Avoidance and ambiguity: Though it is unpleasant to have to deal with a dispute, avoiding a problem will only make it worse. Establish open communication and rational discussion for working on a dispute.

- Forbes contributor and entrepreneur August Turak offers some valuable input on ambiguity and how to increase clarity, especially with a "paper trail" of communications. One key way to avoid ambiguity, he notes, is to be concrete about meeting times and game plans—instead of "maybe," we should use "yes or no" questions and answers whenever possible.
- He also notes that it is important to summarize conflict resolution meetings and have each involved party "sign off" on the summary, indicating that it has been read and agreed upon.[5]

Be firm: Nobody wants to be the "bad guy," but you can be firm without being condescending or mean-spirited.

- Stay calm and have a clear goal for how you woud like the conflict to resolve.

5) August Turak, "The Three Secrets to Conflict Resolution," Forbes, Sept. 10, 2012, retrieved June 26, 2015.

- Balance firmness with directness, honesty and constructive criticism. This will help the receiver be more receptive to your goal (resolving the issue) and it will make your audience respect you more. A leader who can work through problems without resorting to personal attacks is a strong leader who commands appreciation from their colleagues. However, watch out for sugar-coating the situation. It can be confusing. Make sure you are considerate, positive, and constructive.

Dangers of Impersonality and Misunderstandings

Misunderstandings can come in many forms, such as language misunderstandings, cultural miscommunications, and simply from poorly-worded communications. Let's review some common ways that the original message can get lost in translation when writing digitally.

Confusing Wording

When communicating digitally—email or text messaging—it is important to be as clear as possible. Focus your email on one thing only. It is fine to send a second email as a follow-up, or to split a long email into two messages in order to be clear and concise.

Here is an example of two different emails. Which is clearer? Why?

To all in the HR department,

This is a friendly reminder of the meeting that was supposed to be scheduled for next Tuesday but it has been moved to this coming Thursday. This is not to be confused with the board meeting held later that Thursday around 2pm—this one shall be held at 11am.

Please let me know if you have any other questions about either meeting.

Subject: HR meeting Thursday, April 13th, at 2pm.
To all in the HR department,

Though we had planned for a meeting next Tuesday, April 18, we are now going to hold it **this coming Thursday, April 13 at 2pm**. Please mark your calendars and let me know of any conflicts.

[follow-up email]
Subject: Follow-up on board meeting

Furthermore, please keep in mind that the day of the 13th is also the day of our board meeting, which will take place at 11am.

In the first email, the body of the text references three different meetings and no dates for any of them. Somebody is bound to be confused with this wording. The second example is clear about the dates and times, the revised time is bolded, and the follow-up email is specifically about the board meeting.

Again, clarity is the most important thing to keep in mind when writing emails. Not everybody can be on the same page all the time. Getting back on track can be difficult when everybody has different information.

Dates, times, and other things can be misinterpreted unless written clearly, so highlighting any schedule changes you might face with **bolded**, <u>underlined,</u> or *italicized* fonts can help to distinguish what details are being changed.

*Tip: When you have revised a date, place, or instruction about something in an email, you can **bold**, <u>underline,</u> or italicize the changed information so that it is easier to see from a glance.*

Rude Wording

Even though we don't intend to be rude, sometimes our choice of wording can come across as rude if we don't pay attention to how we say things.

Here is another example of how two emails, saying the same thing, can have different meanings depending on their wording.

Adam, You've been warned about missing staff meetings before—this is a written warning. Don't let it happen again. There will be consequences.	Hi Adam, I'm sorry to inform you, but this is a formal, written warning about missing yesterday's mandatory meeting. Please refer to the employee handbook about deadlines and meetings if you are not familiar with the policy. Please let us know ahead of time if you have a foreseeable conflict with any future meetings.

The email on the left is aggressive in tone. It seems as though Adam's supervisor is threatening him. This negatively affects both the employee and the employer on both a professional and emotional level. Depending on the workplace, Adam's supervisor may face issues with harassment in the current wording. This email suggests that he skipped it on purpose, and that is a rude and unprofessional assumption to make.

The email on the right is more direct: it is empathetic, and gives Adam's workplace competence the benefit of the doubt by assuming that he either innocently forgot about the meeting, or that he had a prior appointment at the time of the meeting. This email could be sent after a brief conversation about the issue at hand.

Since written communication takes out many of the subtleties of oral communication (body language, inflections, volume of voice), it is important to write in a manner that is empathetic and sensitive to how people may react to certain words. When writing emails, use an assertive voice. Keep it direct, honest, controlled, empathetic, and constructive.

3.2: Cellphones – Texting and Much, Much More

In the past 20 years, the cellphone has gone from a luxury to an absolute necessity for most people.

The business uses for smartphones today are numerous. However, you need to be careful with how much unnecessary time you spend on your cell or smartphone during the workday.

Using a cell or smartphone when speaking with someone face-to-face is disrespectful, and spending too much time on your cellphone at work could indicate that you are using company time for personal matters.

Text messaging is, generally, a more informal way of communicating within a business setting. You can use text messaging to send quick reminders and updates, and to keep in contact when you are travelling or meeting a colleague somewhere. This is one of the few times you can use very informal writing.

However, some simple guidelines will help you make the most out of this tool:

- Keep your texts brief. Long texts can be difficult to navigate and the reader can lose the point of the message.
- Keep texts work-related. The only texts exchanged while at work should be work-related.
- When in a meeting or other in-person activity, refrain from texting. The focus should be on the people in your presence.
- Use professional tones and word choices when texting.
- If you are using a company phone, be aware of usage. This is company equipment—if you abuse the technology, there can be repercussions.

3.3: Writing Memos

You may have heard the statement, "didn't you see that memo?" If you have never worked in an office before, do you know what a memo really does? When will you need to write one?

Short for *memorandum*, a memo is a brief, one-page communication. It can be a reminder of a due date, meeting, or any other kind of business arrangement. It can also be done to give notice of resignation and to inform management of new employees. It can inform employees of a new policy, or an update to an existing policy. Memos are typically written and distributed to co-workers and management via email.

When to Write a Memo

Memos may be written to either ask staff for or provide them with information.

For example:

An **update memo** informs colleagues and coworkers of events (staff meetings, office lunches, important visitors, special instructions), production deadlines, overhead matters, form signing, and requests for meetings. In some cases, a memo is preferred over an email. For example, if you were leaving a form for a co-worker to sign, or a package to sign for, you may want to include specific instructions for it in a memo attached to the material.

An **inquiry memo** is similar to a survey, and asks the recipients to consider and respond to a request for information.

A **policy memo** informs the recipients of a new policy being instituted.

A **notice-of-change memo** informs employees of a change of staff, policy or process.

Format

When writing a memo, the heading should reflect:

- TO: Readers' name(s), job title(s)
- FROM: Senders' name(s) and job title(s)
- DATE: Month/Day/Year format, or whatever your office prefers
- SUBJECT: Highlights what the memo is about
- BODY PARAGRAPH(S): This is where your message will be—keep it to one page in length

Your subject line should make clear what the matter is about, but it should not be too long. For example, if you were writing a memo about a meeting, it would not be informative enough to have "Meeting" as your subject line. You may want to write, "Meeting about August production deadline."

However, something along the lines of "We will meet on Thursday regarding our August production deadline" is far too wordy for a subject line. You can address the particulars in the body paragraphs of the memo. Like email subject lines, they should be long enough to inform the receiver of exactly what the email is about, but should not be too long.

Usually, a memo should not be longer than one page, though sometimes a longer memo is necessary. For the sake of brevity, one page or less is a fine length for most memo purposes. The body paragraph(s) of your memo should be written clearly. Take a look at this link: **https://owl.english.purdue.edu/owl/resource/590/2/**

As with all business writing, tone of voice is important!

Exercise

Write a memo about the following scenario, using your name as the sender. Keep the body paragraphs brief but informative. Follow each guideline in the scenario.

- You are the sales manager of a small company, and the day is September 28.
- You are going to have a staff meeting on Thursday, October 4, at 11 a.m.
- You have spoken to a client and they have requested to shorten a project deadline to December 15. The deadline was originally dated for January 1.
- The meeting will serve three purposes:
  - to get a progress update from each team.
  - to establish new responsibilities for each team.
  - to establish new strategies to finish the project on time.
- You must be courteous and polite in your language and closing lines
- Consider addressing the new deadline's proximity to the holidays.

my notes

It should look something like this:

TO: All staff
FROM: John Smith, Sales Manager [replace with your name]
DATE: September 28, 2016
SUBJECT: Production deadline meeting on October 4

We will be holding a meeting in the boardroom on Thursday, October 4. I have spoken to our clients, and they wish to shorten the project deadline from January 1 to December 15. Thus, we will need to get a progress report from each team involved in the project, and we will need to establish new responsibilities and strategies to finish the project by then.

I understand that the new deadline is very close to the holiday season, but if we all work together and work efficiently, we will be able to finish the project without any major problems. Please let me know if you cannot make the meeting.

Again, I am confident that the project will be completed timely, and with no problems.

As you see, a memo does not differ much from an email. The medium has simply changed from digital to print. Still, there are certain conventions in sending a memo that you must know so that your communications go smoothly and everybody is on the same page.

Chapter 3 Recap

As we close this chapter, let's look over what we've learned about formatting, tone of voice, and other aspects of communicating properly via email and other written media:

- Being aware of whom you are emailing, and for what purpose, is the most important first step you should take before drafting an email.
- Your subject line is one of the most important parts of an email.
- It should be brief and concise enough to convey the core information of the email, but should leave enough out to prompt the reader to open the email.
- The salutation and closing lines you choose must be appropriate to the person you are emailing.
  - If you don't know the gender or position of the person you are emailing, play it safe and go with "Dear [full name]." You would not want to start an email to a company executive with "Hey, dude."
- Your emails should be short and to the point, using small sentences instead of one large body of text.
  - This is easier to read/digest and looks better on the page.
- Always be empathetic in your tone of voice, and avoid words that others may construe as impatient or rude.
  - This goes for both clients and coworkers—sensitivity goes a long way.
- When working with those from different linguistic and cultural backgrounds from yours, it is important for you to be patient and perceptive of their culture and language skills.
- Conflict resolution, when done through written communications, requires a "paper trail" of the dispute's origin and steps taken to solve it, a free and open manner of discussion, and everyone's interests kept in mind. Again, wording and tone are important.
- You can prevent miscommunications by paying attention to how you organize your thoughts and information in emails.
- Avoid jargon and colloquialisms (especially with clients and coworkers whose first language is not English).

As mentioned early in the chapter, think of the "golden rule" when it comes to proper language for business communications—treat others the way you yourself would like to be treated!

Chapter 3 Quiz

1) Sandra, who works in shipping, and Andrew, who works in quality control, are having a dispute. Sandra claims that Andrew's department has been too slow in getting products to her department, forcing her team to work extra hours. However, she has not been keeping timesheets properly. What would have helped here?

    a. Accountability
    b. A paper trail
    c. More formal email communications
    d. A and B

2) Of the following subject lines, choose the best. The email is a reminder about a meeting.

    a. Meeting April 15th
    b. Sales meeting – Wednesday, April 15, at 2pm
    c. Reminder: Monthly sales meeting on Wednesday, April 15, at 2 p.m.
    d. Do you have a minute to discuss our sales meeting, coming up next Wednesday?

3) What is the best salutation for somebody you have not met or communicated with before?

    a. Dear Sir or Madam,
    b. Greetings,
    c. To whom it may concern,
    d. Dear [full name],

4) True or false: You should write emails in small paragraphs.

Answers:

1. (D) 2. (B) 3. (D) 4. (True)

my notes

Writing in Business

The preceding chapters of this textbook covered the basics of communicating directly with coworkers, clients, and business partners. This chapter focuses on the psychology and mechanics of writing, expanding on the skills needed to prepare technical documentation, persuasive documents, and other forms of professional writing such as proposals, letters, presentations, and reports. The skills reviewed in this chapter are crucial for both writing in business and developing a strong writing presence in your company.

There is certainly a psychology involved in writing for business. This psychology comes both from knowing the audience to whom you are writing, and knowing *how* to write properly in different forms.

Your audience for technical writing can vary. From machinists to medical professionals, or people simply reading instructions for how to put a product together, everybody reading technical writing will need to understand every single step of the process about which you are writing easily. There is an "ideal" you should be able to reach that balances organization with the appropriate level of detail and diction.

A business proposal created to begin a new business relationship with a potential client or partner should be concise, and outline clearly each step of how the project you are proposing *will* unfold, not how it *might* unfold. Expectations and deliverables need to be outlined clearly for both sides.

After this chapter, you will be able to:

Learning Goals

- Understand the assessment, writing, and editing process in full.
- Understand how to tailor your writing for marketing purposes. This includes press releases, white papers, blogging, and social media posts.
- Pay close attention to cultural and linguistic differences when writing for an audience who may not share your first language or cultural norms.
- Understand accountability, professionalism, and ethical concerns with marketing and advertising.
- Write and format both informal and formal proposals and reports properly.

4.1: A Guide to the Writing Process[6]

We have gone over the importance of maintaining an outline and clarity of purpose in your writing, but let's take a closer look. The "AWE" Method, as described by communications writer Janet Mizrahi in her book *Fundamentals of Writing for Marketing and Public Relations*, is a foolproof way to ensure your writing will be on the right track. The writing process moves through three stages—*assess, write*, and *edit*.

Assess Your Process

Before starting a first draft of your piece, consider your audience and purpose. Do this before you begin brainstorming ideas. There are six steps to assess your audience, what kind of language you should use, and how to get your purpose across fully. You can apply these guidelines to any kind of writing, but for the purpose of this chapter, we will focus on how you may apply this process to writing for business communications.

1. Know your audience: This applies to relaying information, the level of diction, and what medium you will use. Your choice matters when you write for marketing and PR purposes.

If someone asks you to write an article focused towards senior citizens as opposed to young people, in which medium would you write? A blog post, tweet, or a newspaper advertisement? Let's look at more details about specific groups of people for whom you may need to write.

- **Age:** Medium, diction, and tone of voice depends on the age group your piece is targeting. Think about how a specific age group may interpret what you are saying.

- **Gender:** If the target gender you are writing for is clearly established, your approach may need to change. However, if your audience is a heterogeneous (mixed-gender) group, you need to allow for this.

- **Language proficiency:** Is your target audience comprised of people whose first language is likely not English? If your audience has a different experience with the language (inexperienced, speaks it as a second language, or speaks a different dialect), write accordingly.

- **Education:** Is your audience university or college-educated? Or is it geared towards people with a high school or elementary school education? As with language proficiency, consider the level of language to use to get your point across by the average education level of your audience.

6) Janet Mizrahi, *Fundamentals of Writing for Marketing and Public Relations: A Step-by-Step Guide for Quick and Effective Results* (New York, NY: Business Expert Press, 2010), 1-14. Web, retrieved 13 July 2015.

- **Knowledge of the topic:** When reading, people are inclined to trust people with a thorough understanding of the topic at hand. Display your qualification to discuss the topic, either explicitly or by suggesting it through the language and expertise you use.

- **Call to action/audience action:** What do you want your audience to do with this material? What point are you trying to make? This depends on the purpose you've chosen for your writing.

2. Define your purpose: Decide if your writing needs to be informative (technical), persuasive (promotional, press, or advertising), or a written request of some kind (a business proposal, a memo, etc.).

- Informative and technical writing needs to follow a step-by-step process. Whether it is assembling a household item (like a blender, or perhaps a television stand), or an industrial machine, be clear about the steps and include the information necessary to complete the process.

- Persuasive writing is used for press releases, grant proposals, white papers, and commercial script writing. It is geared towards promoting a product, or convincing someone of a stance in an argument or debate, or to establish brand loyalty.

- Descriptive writing includes written requests, an invoice for services, a request for a product demonstration or a brochure, or a request to begin a new business relationship. These should be written with the utmost courtesy and clarity. You do not want to sound rude or vague.

3. Brainstorm and research the topic: Brainstorm ideas before beginning to research the topic. A good way to do this is to research keywords on the topic and then gear your thought process to a clear vision of what you want to do with your writing.

- Cite the source for all data, research, and information you use from others. If you do not, you may be accused of plagiarism, which means taking material that is not your own and failing to name the source of the information. This is a serious offence, especially in academic and scientific circles. Note that, depending on the situation, at-work plagiarism can have consequences—up to and including termination.

4. Organize your information: As your research comes together, consider printing all of the material you will use and make notes.

- Highlighting, underlining, and jotting margin notes on data sheets, secondary texts, and other material can prove to be invaluable, especially when you have it all in front of you in print as well as your Word document open on your computer. Recall "Muscle Reading" from chapter 2.

5. Categorize your information into sections: When you have begun taking notes, your initial topics from your brainstorming stage will become clearer and come together logically.

- Think about how you can separate the information you have acquired. Where do things naturally fit the best? Is it easy to read? Do you understand why you chose that order to relay the information?

6. Outline: When creating the outline, ask yourself questions while setting up the categories. What am I talking about? How does it connect to the topic or purpose? Why is this important or being included? What else could happen or has happened?

You can apply these steps to any type of writing from a memo, to a business proposal or white paper, or emails to colleagues and clients. It is always important to know what kind of language to use and to establish a clear, logical flow.

my notes

....
....
....
....
....
....
....
....

"The first sentence can't be written until the last sentence is written."

- Joyce Carol Oates, author of A Garden of Earthly Delights

Writing Stage

Now that you have established a logical flow for your writing, you can write the first draft. Remember, your first draft is just that: a draft. You will have opportunities to alter them during the editing stage. Using your outline as the starting point, expand on the points in your outline to create sentences and paragraphs.

The first draft is, above all, a way to get your thoughts, ideas, and logical flow onto paper or a computer document. Let's look at the editing stage next.

Editing Stage

Editing is time-consuming and can be very frustrating, but it is essential for creating a strong piece of writing.

No first draft will ever be perfect. The editing stage is your opportunity to add and remove content so your writing is relevant, concise, and engaging.

Global editing involves looking at the piece as a whole. This means you will print your draft, review to ensure you have covered the core concepts, and assess how effectively you laid out the topics and their supporting facts. This stage is mostly where you will double check that your audience and purpose are compatible to your overall piece.

> "The first draft is just you telling yourself the story."
>
> - Terry Pratchett, author of the Discworld series

Do this before getting into **local editing**, which takes a much closer examination at your sentence and paragraph structure, your word choice, and the grammar you use throughout your piece.

Keep a grammar guide handy (the first chapter of this book would work), as well as a thesaurus, at every step of local editing. This stage helps you ensure that your pronoun use is correct, your subject-verb order is agreeable throughout the text, and that you are using the active voice where possible, among many other important grammar rules.

Each paragraph should focus on one idea. Every sentence in a paragraph should relate to the topic of that paragraph. Evaluate your word choice and look at either refining details and examples or adding/deleting them. Details and examples should be specific and relatable.

In terms of *paragraph length*, a paragraph should be four to five sentences—or, if you are writing for a lower reading level, three sentences would suffice. If the paragraph is longer than five sentences, consider breaking it into two or more paragraphs.

The desired sentence length is debatable and depends on the context of your writing. Long paragraphs broken up into smaller chunks of sentences are often more visually appealing and easier to digest than long-winded blocks of sentences. You'll reach a wider audience if your prose is visually appealing as well as engaging. Remember, the reach of your message is as important as the message itself.

You should edit your draft a few times. Pay attention to flow, visual arrangement, and how your points are coming across. Once you work out the details, you can move on to the second step of editing your draft.

Proofreading is all about focusing on correcting the grammar, punctuation, and spelling. Most companies that work chiefly with writing—marketing firms, websites, and newspapers—will have a proofreader on staff. Regardless, you must still proofread your work yourself. You should have a paper copy of your document on hand so you can mark any errors.

Protip:
The spellcheckers on software like Microsoft Word and Google Docs won't catch everything and are far

from foolproof—be careful using them and always use your common sense and understanding of grammar.

4.2: Writing Persuasively Using the Active Voice

When writing for business—especially when writing proposals, plans, formal and informal reports—writing in the active voice is important. Writing in the active voice means that the subject of the sentence *performs* the action.

Here are some examples of sentences in the active and passive voices.

Passive Voice: The car was driven by Mark to the meeting.
Active Voice: Mark drove the car to the meeting.

Passive Voice: It is believed by Caroline that the schedules should be re-written.
Active Voice: Caroline believes that the schedules should be re-written.

Passive Voice: The fish was cooked perfectly by the chef.
Active Voice: The chef cooked the fish perfectly.

As you see in these examples, many times the passive voice uses the word *by*. The second example is particularly awkward, but by simply putting the subject in front of the action of the sentence, and changing the tense of the verb "believe," the sentence is much easier to read.

Being clear and concise is important for communicating in a business environment. It is a small change to make to your writing, but using the active voice will make it much stronger.

Exercise

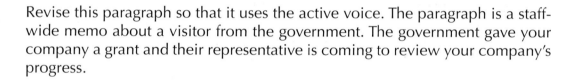

Revise this paragraph so that it uses the active voice. The paragraph is a staff-wide memo about a visitor from the government. The government gave your company a grant and their representative is coming to review your company's progress.

FROM: Mohammed Faizan, Assistant to the CEO
TO: All staff
DATE: April 3, 2016
SUBJECT: Government inspection next week

To all staff,

Regarding our recent funding grant, our office will be visited by a government representative to oversee how our grant money has been budgeted in the past month. The government representative will be arriving at 3pm on Wednesday, April 10, next week.

Please make sure that your desks are cleaned by you, and that you are to be dressed appropriately for our office being visited. Ensure you will be in the office, and do not hesitant to ask any further questions.

Best regards,
Mohammed Faizan

my notes

....

....

....

....

....

....

....

....

Though Mohammed's style is consistent, it is awkward to read in the passive voice. A revised version should look like this:

FROM: Mohammed Faizan, Assistant to the CEO
TO: All staff
DATE: April 3, 2016
SUBJECT: Government inspection next week

To all staff,

Regarding our recent funding grant, a government representative will visit us next week to oversee our progress and budget. We are expecting the representative's arrival at 3pm on Wednesday, April 10, next week.

Please make sure your desks and all common areas are clean, and that you dress appropriately for their visit. Ensure that you are present in the office, and do not hesitate to ask me any further questions.

Best regards,
Mohammed Faizan

When written in the active voice, the memo is much clearer to read, much stronger, and more urgent. Being assertive in your writing ensures that all of your co-workers understand your purpose.

4.3: Intercultural Correspondence

Being able to communicate with clients and colleagues from cultures other than your own is important.

One key concept to keep in mind is ethnocentrism. Ethnocentrism is the idea that one culture or social group is more important or superior to others. While you may not actually believe this, you can suggest it without meaning to with some of your actions or words.

You run the risk of offending people and other cultures if you are not careful, especially in your written communications.

One-on-One Communications

Cultural differences are a major hurdle you will face when dealing with co-workers, clients, and anyone else whose first language or culture is not the same as your own.

Here are a few key things to keep in mind when corresponding with clients and colleagues. People from other cultures working together brings fresh perspectives, new talents, and a stronger office culture all around. Thus, it is important to be respectful and empathetic when engaging with those from cultural backgrounds that are not your own.

Be patient
- Be patient and courteous when communicating with people whose first language is not yours, or those who come from a different cultural background.

- When communicating in person or by email, ensure you do not use jargon or terms that a non-native English speaker would find difficult to understand.

- Use short sentences, short paragraphs, and avoid abbreviations. Mistranslations and miscommunications can easily occur this way.

- Ensure you don't make your language overly simple—this could lead to insulting someone's intelligence. If you have never communicated with that person before, assume they have at least a beginner's grasp of the language, and gauge your communications from there. Allow your client or co-worker to ask questions, and, if necessary, request a translator for assistance.

Did you know?
In Japan, it is customary to receive a business card with both hands and a bowing gesture. The Japanese consider it extremely rude not to do this. This is one of many things to keep in mind when doing business with others.

Pay attention to different cultural norms: Not everyone shares your cultural values, manners, and standards. This is very important to recognize when working with foreign clients. Diversity is what makes us all interesting, and everybody brings something to the table.

- Different cultures have different views on hierarchy, power, and how you should address superiors.

- In many Western office cultures, disagreements between subordinates and superiors (within reason) are often encouraged. However, as an example, Japanese business culture holds authority and hierarchy in very high regard. They consider it very disrespectful to challenge a superior on a decision. For foreign clients and colleagues, be sure you are aware of what type of power the person you are addressing holds.

- Be wary of words and wording that others may consider offensive or prejudiced.

- Be aware of how other cultures interpret eye contact and other aspects of body language.

- Be aware of personal space and other personal preferences that can lead to offense if infringed.

This also pertains to cultural-specific phrases and words. For example, how would a person in India, where baseball is not as popular as in Canada and the US, reply to the phrase "touch base," or "ballpark figure?"

We all need to play a part in making our offices inclusive, equitable, and free from prejudice, oppressive behaviour, and cultural insensitivity.

Avoid Slang and Colloquialisms

Though English is one of the most widely spoken languages in the world, and one of the world's main business languages, not everyone speaks it fluently, or comes from the same regional dialect or cultural background.

Many things about the English language can get lost in translation—**slang** and **colloquialisms** are among them. *Colloquialisms* are figures of speech, often country or region-specific, that often do not translate into other languages.

Here is a brief list of North American colloquialisms to avoid typing in emails to foreign clients or colleagues. There are many more, of course, but these are popular ones you may use in business communications.

- *ballpark figure*: an estimate of a number

  It's a ballpark figure of around $20 million.
  Clearer: We have an estimated cost of around $20 million.

- *nailed it*: someone did well on something

  Great job on that presentation, you really nailed it.
  Clearer: You did a great job on that presentation.

- *icing on the cake:* an added bonus to something already good

  And the icing on the cake is that we did better than our projected figures.
  Clearer: Even better, we made more money than what we thought we would.

- *touch base:* keep informed of news and updates

  Let's touch base tomorrow afternoon.
  Clearer: Let's discuss this matter further tomorrow afternoon.

- *make a rain check:* reschedule a cancelled appointment.

  I'm sorry, I have to cancel our meeting tomorrow.
  Let's make a rain check for next Monday.
  Clearer: I'm sorry, I have to cancel our meeting tomorrow.
  Let's re-schedule for next Monday.

When you look at colloquialisms laid out in a list like this, you can certainly see how they may confuse someone whose first language is not English, or if they are not originally from North America.

Being aware of the level of language you are using with foreign coworkers and clients will ensure that you both understand each other clearly.

Slang is when we create new meaning for words or create new words. We often use slang in informal settings, and it can vary based on the geographic location, group of people, and the context in which we use them. While we use slang most often in speech rather than in writing, it is important to be able to distinguish it when it is used.

Just like colloquialisms, slang can lead to confusion during communication if not all parties are familiar with it. To compound the problem, slang words are often created and used for a short time only. They are usually tied to pop culture.

> Could you grab me a double-double?
> Is the plan cool with you?
> Since the weather is a little dicey, I won't go today.
> Could you lend me a couple of bucks to buy lunch.

To avoid the confusion that can arise with using slang, it is best to avoid using it altogether, especially in written business communication.

Professionalism and Ethics

Ethics are a crucial part of any profession, and this is no different in a business setting. Applied ethics are codes of right and wrong conduct that someone in a specific situation must uphold. Part of *professionalism*, or conducting yourself in a professional and courteous manner, is paying attention to professional and personal ethics in your life and work. There will be times in your career when you might face a decision that could affect your integrity, or how others see you. In cases like this, it is important to act ethically.

Examples of applied ethics include medical conduct (the Hippocratic Oath), obeying legal conduct codes (in Ontario, the Law Society of Upper Canada establishes these), and many other frameworks of right and wrong behaviour and conduct.

Professional ethics in a business sense include, but are not limited to, ethical concerns in advertising and discriminatory business practices on both small and larger scales. Let's look at how to be professional and ethical regarding these issues.

Discrimination

Discrimination is the unfair treatment of people based on their gender, sexual orientation, race, creed, age, ability, or social status.

Discrimination can be seen and done either explicitly (racist or sexist slurs, workplace harassment), or more subtly, like hiring processes and promotions where one group of people may be favoured over another. Discriminatory practices undermine the integrity of a business' culture, and, more importantly, harms individuals and social groups.

In Ontario, there is legislation in place to prevent discriminatory practices in the workplace. The Ontario Human Rights Commission (OHRC) is an agency—independent of Ontario's provincial government—that upholds and advances the *Human Rights Code* through public inquiry, policymaking, and the Human Rights Tribunal, where the agency mediates formal complaints between an individual and accused party. Here are the protected grounds and areas for discrimination in Ontario.

Protected Grounds	Protected Areas
• Age • Ancestry/colour/race • Citizenship • Ethnic origin • Place of origin • Creed (beliefs) • Disability • Family status • Marital status • Gender identity, expression • Receipt of public assistance • Record of public offenses • Sex (breastfeeding, pregnancy) • Sexual orientation	• Accommodation • Contracts • Employment • Goods, services, and facilities • Membership in trade or professional associations, or unions

Did you know?
The Hippocratic Oath, written by the Greek philosopher Hippocrates in the 5th century BCE, is one of the oldest ethical codes in history.

4.4: Reports and Proposals[7]

In many situations, you will be writing to a specific, well-defined audience regarding a specific topic.

Proposals for new business deals, grant applications, and reports for ongoing projects, are all examples of reports someone might ask you to write. A report or a proposal may be informal or formal, depending on your audience. Informal reports and formal reports each have their own specific format, structure, and style expected by its audience.

Informal Reports

An effective business report always has one clear objective. A report is not a platform of opinion, but an impartial communication of facts to your audience.

Before writing a report, ask yourself two questions:

> 1. Was the reader aware of the issue before?

or

> 2. Is the issue something new that has come to light?

Informal reports come in the form of memos, sales reports, and daily progress reports. An informal report is typically short, and speaks to a focused question or task. There are two kinds of informal reports: the informational report and the analytical report.

An **informational report** is a routine report summarizing the fact of a situation or process. You use this kind of report to compile data and get a general feeling for how a process or project is going.

You use an **analytical report** to solve a problem, analyze a situation, and recommend a course of action to solve that problem or situation. These reports can be very challenging to write, as they require lots of in-depth research and analysis of findings and facts.

7) Margot Northey and Joan McKibbin, *Impact! A Guide to Business Communication*, Pearson Canada Inc. (Toronto: 2012), 111-67.

Elements of an Informal Report

Format an informal report so it is easy to read. The following guidelines should make a report easier for you to write, and for your reader to follow.

- **Purpose:** Open your report with a statement of purpose. The best way to open a report is simply "This report examines/addresses…" or something along those lines.

- **Key points:** Include a paragraph of key points following your purpose.

- **Discussion of findings:** After offering a short preview of your key points, review your key points in more detail.

  - This is how you will arrange your facts to lead to your conclusion or recommendations.
  - Organize them in order of their importance to the report, and divide the report into the relevant sections.
  - Use headings and subheadings to organize where and when you will discuss your findings.
    - Put all relevant information into the categories (headings) you have planned.
    - Don't let information overlap into other categories.
    - Keep the amount of information in each category consistent.

- **Order of report:** Depending on the topic and context of your report, you will need to structure your report in different ways. Three possible methods of organising your information are:

  - **Chronological order:** If you are arranging information and findings into time periods, arrange it in the order it occured.
  - **Spatial order:** This kind of order works best when you are working with different locational or geographical data. For example, if you were comparing sales in different cities, you would have one heading per city, and arrange your findings in each.
  - **Comparison:** If you are weighing the merits of two or more things, for example, comparing fuel mileage for two or more different cars, arrange your findings to compare these numbers.

- **Conclusion:** An informational report usually has a conclusion. An analytical report has a list of recommendations at the end.

No matter which layout you use for a report, make it visually appealing to read. Headings and subheadings will be crucial for this—when you format your headings and subheadings, they need to be consistent.

Formal Reports

A **formal report** is typically longer and involves more research than an informal report. The "four Rs" of planning a formal report are:

1. *Reason* for writing
2. Information about the *Receiver*
3. *Restrictions*
4. *Research* involved with your project

Your restrictions are important to identify. Establish them right away.

Consider the following when planning your research:

- **Finances:** What kind of budget and expenses do you have for this project?

- **Personnel:** How many people will you require for the project? What kind of professional services? Will you need to contract from outside?

- **Time:** What is the deadline of the project? It is helpful to impose your own dates on the different stages of the project so that you can factor in margins of error and delays.

my notes

....

....

....

....

....

....

....

....

....

Protip:
Though formal reports are much more impersonal than informal reports, you will still want to use personal pronouns such as "I" and "we." At one time, it was common practice to omit personal pronouns, but this is now considered out of date.

Elements of a Formal Report

The structure of a formal report, and the detail of what you should cover in each section, is as follows:

- **Front section**
    - Title page
    - Letter of transmittal
    - Table of contents

- **Main section**
    - Summary
    - Introduction
    - Discussion of findings
    - Conclusions and recommendations

- **Back section**
    - References
    - Appendix

Title Page: Your title page should be the first page of the document. Include:

- The title of the report (in boldface, capital letters, or a larger font than the rest of the text)
- The name and title of the reader
- The writer's name and title, or the name of the firm
- The date the report was finished

Letter of Transmittal: The **letter of transmittal** refers to the text you use to introduce yourself, your team, and your project, to the receiver of your report. You can use this in both intra-office and inter-office reports. A letter of transmittal should offer a quick overview of your project or proposal. This letter should always be very formal and concise. The tone you take in your letter will affect how the receiver reads the rest of your report.

Summary: The main section of a formal report is a summary addressing the report's key points. It is also referred to as an executive summary—a condensed overview of what the report will go over in further detail. Write the executive summary after you complete the whole report.

Be brief in this summary: use lists when possible, don't use too many examples or other supporting details, and stay close to the facts. Your summary may be the only thing that they look at initially, so keep it concise and easy to read.

Introduction: Elaborates on the process established by the report's summary. It may have several subheadings or sections. Ensure your introduction includes the following components:

- **Purpose:** Describe your intent for writing in a concise, one sentence explanation.
- **Background:** This section explains the reason the report is required and the conditions that have influenced the situation.
- **Scope:** Establish any constraints or boundaries in the direction of your investigation to ensure the limitations are clear to the audience and avoid misunderstandings.
- **Method:** Outline the steps you took to compile the data in the report. This can be through either "soft" data (surveys, questionnaires, et cetera), or more technical, quantifiable data (such as sales figures). It depends on what kind of report you are writing.

Discussion of Findings: The **discussion of findings** immediately follows the introduction. This section will be the longest part of your report, reviews the points in your introduction, and will discuss the facts on which you have based your conclusion or final recommendations in detail. You need to separate your findings into logical headings and subheadings. These sections should be concise, including all the relevant information.

Conclusions/Recommendations: Your conclusions and recommendations should close the report. **Conclusions** are the results and inferences of your findings. **Recommendations** are the suggested actions the company or individual(s) should take, based on the findings and conclusions of the report.

Back Section: The back section of your formal report should include your **references** and an **appendix** if you require one. References are what you use to cite information that is uncommon knowledge or something you borrowed from other sources. You must properly cite all information that is not yours. Otherwise, it could be considered plagiarism.[8]

Appendix: (plural: appendices) Used to document highly specialized language or nonessential information that could prove to be important or interesting to the reader.

8) *Plagiarism occurs when you do not properly cite information you use that is not your own. Determine which format your organization uses: APA (American Psychological Association), MLA (Modern Language Association), Chicago Style, or Harvard Style.*

Use appendices for tables, charts, and other technical information that is relevant to your report's findings, but not essential to actually reading the report. Appendices help reduce visual clutter and make the report more readable, so the reader can focus on the report's essential information.

Exercise

Write a proper letter of transmittal using the following criteria:

- You work for a small company that produces ergonomic chairs. You have been given $25,000 to produce a new chair design for people with lower back problems.

- Your team spent $10,000 on research, $5,000 on design materials, and $10,000 on labour costs across a three-month period.

- Your report, as a whole, is about the design and production of the chair, but your letter of transmittal focuses on the budget. You will discuss the budget in detail in the report, but there is a brief overview in the letter of transmittal.

- The name of the person you are addressing is Andrea Laviolette, and she is the CEO of your company. You may address her by her first name.

- Your letter of transmittal should be three paragraphs:
  - Paragraph #1: Introduce the report.
  - Paragraph #2: Discuss the budget numbers and where you allocated them.
  - Paragraph #3: Thank Andrea for her time and inform her that you look forward to her feedback.

....
....
....
....
....
....

When completed, it should look something like this:

> Dear Andrea,
>
> Attached is the report you requested on our latest chair project. The enclosed report covers the budgetary matters, design conception, and prototype building we have worked on for the past three months. Though we will report on the budget more in-depth further in the report, we have prefaced the report with a brief overview for your convenience.
>
> As per the budget: we allocated $10,000 to ergonomic research to make a chair to ease lower back problems, $5000 on materials to make our initial prototype, and $10,000 on labour costs for our team to conduct research, draft a design, and build the prototype.
>
> We look forward to hearing your feedback on our work. Please don't hesitate to ask any questions you may have.
>
> Best regards,
> [Your name]

As you see, the letter of transmittal has done two important things: it has responded appropriately to the request for the report, and established exactly what the report is about and why the receiver will find it important. Your receiver will not want to read the whole report before understanding what the report is about, so it is important to get your introductory letter right.

Proposals[9]

Proposals can be internal or external and can be as simple as a one-page memo, or as involved as a large document written to a government agency or another company. They can be solicited or unsolicited, but you usually write them in response to a request for proposal (RFP).

You use internal proposals for situations such as expenditures or policy changes. In contrast, you use external proposals to propose new business deals with other companies as well as for marketing purposes.

As with all business writing, regardless of how long or formal the proposal is, you have to keep your audience and purpose in mind throughout the writing process. Has the proposal been *solicited* through an RFP? Are you trying to sell a service to a company or request services for your own company?

If your proposal is *unsolicited,* it will need to be more convincing than if someone requested it. Regardless, if you are trying to sell a product or service externally or propose changes to policy and expenditures, your proposal is for your reader.

9) Margot Northey and Joan McKibbin, *Impact! A Guide to Business Communication,* Pearson Canada Inc. (Toronto: 2012) 160-7

Structure of a Proposal

The basic outline of a proposal organizes the document so it is easy to read, easy to scan, and the information flows logically from the statement of its purpose to its conclusion.

- **Method:** Outline the method you will use, limiting your use of technical language.
  - After you have done this, you can get into more detail about exactly how you will go about the process.
  - This is a good time to inform any specialists in the organization you are addressing of any technical requirements.

- **Time frame:** If time is going to be a condition of your project, mention the estimated time of each stage of the project.

- **Cost:** How much your project is going to cost is an important factor for yourself and the company, department, or consultant you are working with. Here are a few things to be aware of when writing your cost expectations:
  - Is it an estimate or a competitive price that is a selling point for your proposal? Don't be afraid to mention if you do not have a projected cost. It is best to be transparent in a proposal.
  - If you are doing a larger proposal for an outside party, outline the cost for each stage of the project. This makes it easier for the contractor to read and allocate funds more freely.

- **Qualifications:** Why are you and your company qualified to take on this project?
  - At this stage of the proposal, your heading should emphasize your qualifications. Include contact information about each person involved in the project, and attach résumés.

- **Benefits:** What will you and your reader gain from your proposal?
  - Make this as clear as possible at the end of the proposal. Outline how it may affect productivity, save the client money, or anything else that the proposal seeks to accomplish for the reader.

Business Plans[10]

Business plans are similar to proposals, but you need to be more in-depth about your own company, its process, and its long-term goals. You will usually write a business plan when applying for a grant, venture capital, or a bank loan. Avoid using jargon when writing your business plan. Your audience may not be as business-savvy as you are, and they need to understand who you are, what you do, and what the end goal is for both you and their investment.

The basic structure of a business plan is as follows:

- **Executive summary:** Like a formal report, your executive summary should offer an overview of the key points of your plan. It is usually the first section an investor reads, so be interesting, concise, and accurate.

- **Business strategy:** Outline what your business does and how it does it.
    - **Overview:** Review the history of your business and its purpose. Describe your products/services and the legal structure of your business.
    - **Current position:** At what stage of your business' life cycle are you? What have you achieved?
    - **Competitive advantage:** Include details on your competitors, your business model, and what your company has to offer.
    - **Growth plan:** Where does your company see itself in five years? Go over any milestones and goals for the future in this section.

- **Marketing strategy:** Consider the "four Ps," your marketing budget, and a profile of your ideal customers. The four Ps are product, price, placement, and promotion.

- **Operational plan:** Outline your company's daily operations, what kind of facility requirements you need/use, management information, and information technology (IT) systems.

- **Strengths, weaknesses, opportunity, and threat analysis (SWOT):** Be realistic about your business goals. Some situations will arise that are out of your control. Addressing these situations in a risk assessment indicates that you have considered them in an objective way.

10) Government of Canada, "Writing your business plan," Canada Business Network, last modified September 9, 2014. http://www.canadabusiness.ca/eng/page/2753/&r=1/#rte

- **Human resources plan:** Outline how you plan to manage your employees, both short-term and long-term.
  - It may help to offer an overview of your staff, what each department does, how your training program works, and other important personnel information.

- **Social responsibility strategy:** Social responsibility gives you a competitive advantage by putting a good "face" on your company. Your ethical values will feature in this section. Include any fair-trade certifications, community achievements, or environmental accolades.

- **E-Business strategy:** How do you plan to use Internet technologies and communications within your business? Discuss web development, technology specialists you will use, et cetera.

- **Financial forecasts:** Include a forecast of three to five years, with the most detail for the first 12 months.
  - Include cash flow statements, a profit and loss forecast, and a sales forecast.
  - Cover various scenarios and include a contingency plan for any risks.

- **Exit strategy:** How you plan to leave your business, when the time comes, is an important thing to address to investors, planners, and possible business partners. Close your plan with this section.

You can tailor this structure to fit your particular needs. However, remember your audience is expecting a certain format and will expect to see specific information in certain places within the proposal. Too much creative liberty will distract readers and the plan will be more difficult to read.

my notes

....

....

....

....

....

....

....

....

Chapter 4 Recap

As we close this chapter, let's go over the takeaway points:

- Begin your writing process by considering your audience, purpose, and how you will conduct research.

- You will brainstorm, and then organize your information—including creating an outline to ensure you are covering all the key points.

- You will then begin writing your first draft.

- Once you finish the first draft, you will revise and proofread your message in separate steps to ensure you capture all the details.

- Write using the active voice, with positive language, varied sentence structure, and language and tone appropriate to your audience and topic.

- Communicating with people from different cultures requires patience, attention to different cultural norms, and language free from slang and colloquialisms.

- Ethics are important for business—treat people with equity and be honest in all your communications with colleagues, clients, and suppliers, alike.

- Informal reports (analytical and informational) are usually internal, short, and routine pieces of writing you will need to create.

- Formal reports are longer, more detailed, and produced for internal or external audiences. They are written for a very specific purpose.

- Proposals can be either solicited or unsolicited, and give a concise, detailed outline of a plan of action.

- Business plans require you to go into very specific detail of how your company operates, its goals and future plans, and social responsibility, among many other factors.

Chapter 4 Quiz

1) What would you call a region-specific phrase that does not translate well into other languages?

    a. Contraction
    b. Ballpark figure
    c. Colloquialism
    d. Branding

2) What is Ontario's anti-discrimination body, independent of the provincial government?

    a. Better Business Bureau
    b. Ministry of Labour
    c. Governor General
    d. Ontario Human Rights Commission

3) True or false: the passive voice is preferred in business writing.

4) What is an executive summary?

5) Why is referencing (or citing) sources important?

6) What kind of writing is routine, and one that businesses usually use to convey information internally?

    a. Proposals
    b. Informal report
    c. Formal report
    d. Business plan

7) What should be the longest part of a formal report?

a. Executive summary
b. Appendix
c. Discussion of findings
d. Business plan

8) What is plagiarism?

a. Ethical behaviour
b. A form of writing
c. Failing to cite the source of a thought or idea that is not your own
d. Not important in business writing

9) What is discrimination?

a. A way to determine our audience
b. Not an issue in current business
c. Unfair treatment of individuals based on gender, age or other defining attributes
d. Always direct and obvious

10) What is a business plan?

a. An internal document
b. A document used to apply for a grant or loan
c. An informal document
d. Not used in the business world

Answers:

1. (C) 2. (D) 3. (false) 4. (A condensed overview of the key points of a formal report) 5. (to avoid plagiarism.) 6. (B) 7. (C) 8. (C) 9. (C) 10. (B)

my notes

Developing Oral Communication Skills

The first four chapters of this textbook covered the skills and information surrounding written communications applicable to communicating with others in a business environment. This chapter discusses the other major aspect of professional business communication: oral communication. To begin, this chapter focuses on developing and applying professional oral communication skills.

The ability to engage in effective oral communication, by speaking clearly and concisely, is important in your professional life. Ineffective oral communication skills in business can come at a high cost: lost contracts, promotions, clients, or even your own job.

For example, when talking with potential clients regarding important business dealings, you want to make accurate assessments of the clients' needs are, even if they are unspoken. Conducting professional oral communication requires using accepted rules on verbal etiquette, active listening, nonverbal signals, and the scope of communication across different cultures.

Learning Goals

- Utilize active listening skills and respond in an appropriate manner.
- Understand the elements that comprise verbal etiquette.
- Improve your speeches and meetings through developing public speaking techniques.
- Identify nonverbal communication signals and understand the importance of their role in communication.
- Account for issues such as cultural differences and ensure the message remains the same even when engaging in intercultural communication.
- Comprehend the benefits of positive communication and the potentially detrimental effects of negative communication.

my notes

5.1: Active Listening

We listen to messages around us in several ways, and some are more effective than others. **Passive listening** is allowing the words and message to pass through you without truly listening to when someone is speaking. It is one of the most common forms of listening, and is also the least effective method.

Selective listening—or only listening for key words—is another common and ineffective listening technique. Essentially, you only hear what you want to hear, and begin formulating your reply before the speaker finishes. You want to learn active listening skills instead.

Active listening is the process through which the listener captures the speaker's entire message by listening for both the words and emotions. It is composed of three components: receiving the message, processing the message, and responding to the message.

The listener provides feedback through nodding, consistent eye contact, and paraphrasing the speaker's words afterwards to ensure that they received the correct message. As a listener actively engaging in this process, you are demonstrating that you understand the complete meaning of the message.

This three-component process of receiving, processing, and responding to the message confirms that all parties understand the discussion.

Conflict resolution makes use of active listening. It minimizes the potential for misunderstandings because the listener must verify the speaker's meaning prior to responding. There are four main things to keep in mind when you are trying to become an active listener:

1. Pay attention to the speaker.
2. Make it clear that you are listening to them.
3. Do not interrupt while they are speaking.
4. Provide appropriate feedback after the speaker is finished.

Preparing to Actively Listen

Before a conversation starts, make the commitment to participate as an active listener.

First, stop all activities you might be doing, unless they are relevant to the conversation. This means you should not have any distractions like computer or phone screens in the way of the conversation. Turn off the monitor, put the phone away, and focus your attention on the speaker. However, it is acceptable to take notes during a business conversation as an element of active listening.

Active listening does not include wearing headphones: be respectful and take them off!

Additionally, review what you already know about the speaker and the upcoming topic before the conversation gets going. If you are preparing for a business meeting, review any information you have on the topics so you are well informed. Make notes during the meeting so you capture the information you need. Prepare questions to ask the audience, and anticipate questions you may be asked. If you can, have answers prepared for those questions so you are not caught off-guard.

Finally, be aware of and keep separate any emotional responses regarding the subject, including any opinions and prejudices. The focus should remain on the speaker for the duration of the conversation until the time you are able to give a response. Also, consider any emotional, hot button points of the topic that the speaker may have in order to avoid misphrasing a comment and creating conflict.

During The Conversation

When the conversation or meeting begins, you have a number of tasks as an active listener.

- Focus on the person who is speaking. Listen for the spoken message and word choice. Also watch for the non-verbal cues, such as their body language (gestures, posture, eye contact), and tone of voice. Realize that people will put more faith in body language and the non-verbal cues than in your actual words.

- Maintain consistent and appropriate eye contact with the speaker, along with engaging in some non-verbal signals, like a smile or head nod, to communicate to them that you are paying attention to their words. Be aware that eye contact in different cultures can communicate different meanings, and what is appropriate in North America may be rude in another part of the world.

- Do not interrupt the speaker while they are talking to you. Always let the conversation run its course and wait until the speaker asks you to respond, whether it is through inviting questions or asking for input on an issue.

- Verify that you understand the speaker's meaning, whether it was made clear or only suggested, by paraphrasing or asking questions. This ensures correct reponses to the speaker. A simple misinterpretation of what the speaker might have meant can result in a misunderstanding and eventual conflict between the involved parties.

Easy Steps to Follow

To ensure you understand the speaker's message, follow these three steps:

1. **Ask Open Ended Questions:** Rather than looking for short yes or no answers to your question (e.g. Did that make you feel frustrated?), try rephrasing questions to get the speaker to explain their point in detail, as in, "Why did that situation frustrate you?"

2. **Summarize:** When the speaker is finished talking, try briefly summarizing what they said to verify what they meant. An example of this would be saying something such as the following: "To summarize, the busy days at your job have been causing you a lot of stress, but you still enjoy your work and don't wish to leave."

3. **Respond:** You want to respond to the speaker in a considerate manner, while remaining objective and focused on the message. Take the time to process what they said, what they intended with the message, and then respond to the message. For instance, if the speaker was describing a difficult situation, they are likely frustrated. That might be evident in their words, tone, or body language. Frame your response with a statement like, "that must have been difficult," to help diffuse some of that emotion. Watch your tone so you do not come across as sarcastic or condescending. This demonstrates to the other person you were listening to the entire message.

Benefits of Active Listening

Utilizing active listening skills is critical in the workplace. It demonstrates that you are attentive to others when they are speaking and conveying their message. Verifying that you understand the message before responding reduces misunderstandings and conflict.

Active listening:

- Demonstrates respect to the speaker.
- Encourages the speaker to open up.
- Results in fewer misunderstandings.
- Promotes improved negotiation between the involved parties.
- Promotes heightened motivation to complete tasks.
- Saves lots of time and money.
- Encourages participants to see potential/current problems and start to work on solving them within one conversation.
- Reduces the need for repeating conversations later.

Consider the amount of time you can save using active listening skills, and how you can dedicate that time to other projects, or even progressing further on the issue if there are additional elements that require discussion beyond the initial conversation.

Example of Active Listening

1.

Speaker: I just don't know what everyone expects of me! Tomorrow I have to go over 15 job applications and devise a basic set of interview questions for all of them, as well as individualizing questions based on their specific qualifications and experiences. I'm only one individual and I have so many other things to do before I leave for my vacation.

They want to have a new person hired by the end of next week. It does not give me a lot of time to conduct interviews in a way I am happy with and send out an offer before I go on vacation. I mean, I know that I can get this done, but seriously? They have to know that it's a lot for one person to handle.

2.

Listener: From my understanding, you are feeling stressed out about the short time frame you have to get all of this work done, but you still enjoy what you do.

3.

Speaker: That's exactly it. I am sure that I will get this done. I am good at my job, but it is definitely still stressful. I might need to call on people to help, but everything will work out.

4.

Listener: Let me know how things are going and if there is anything I can do to help you do your job effectively.

5.

Speaker: I will. Thanks for listening.

In this conversation, the listener waited to respond to the speaker until there was a natural ending to what they had to say: they did not interrupt in the middle. Additionally, they designed an appropriate response that summarizes what the speaker was saying while taking care to avoid offending anyone by making an inference about what the speaker might be feeling. The speaker feels heard, and now the two can go on to solve the current issue.

Exercise

In the following scenario, how would you respond to the speaker while demonstrating active listening techniques? Exchange with a partner and compare your responses.

> "I have a couple job offers from two great companies. One is in this city, but the other is a few hours away so I would have to move. The one here offers higher pay and some basic benefits, but the other one is closer to what I want to do for the rest of my life. But it doesn't offer me as much money and I don't know anyone in that city."

my notes

....
....
....
....
....
....
....
....
....
....
....
....
....
....
....
....

Be Wary of Selective Listening

One of the most common methods of listening is selective listening. Selective listening filters information into key thoughts or words, and does not catch the whole message. It is only hearing what you want to hear, without comprehending other points made during a conversation.

Selective listening appears as:

- **Multitasking:** Most commonly, multitasking is engaging in other activities while someone is talking, such as reading documents or watching videos. Planning what you are going to say before a speaker finishes is also multitasking. Do not jump to a conclusion as someone is speaking, disregarding the rest of the message. This is not an effective method for listening.

- **Filtering:** In selective listening, filtering is deciding what is most important, even before a speaker is finished, and only trying to retain that information—letting everything else fall to the wayside.

In business, selective listening is detrimental to effective daily activities. Selective listening often causes misunderstandings and missing important information due to distractions from the conversation at hand. Consequences can include:

- Damaged relationships with co-workers and/or clients
- Cancellation of contracts (loss of business)
- Extra work required to rectify a situation
- Incurring extra costs if you must issue replacements or refunds

5.2: Verbal Etiquette

Your workplace conversations should always be calm, respectful, and fruitful, regardless of the topic. **Verbal etiquette** ensures all involved parties remain objective and focused on the issues, not the emotions, in order to prevent any misunderstandings. Following a few simple rules helps ensure that no one will feel disrespected.

Stay calm with others, even if you are upset.

Think Before You Speak

There can be negative consequences for the simple mistake of not taking a moment to think before you speak. This is especially important during arguments. Take the time to form a response and keep patience and empathy in mind.

Listen While You Speak

Active listening is important when someone else is speaking, but did you know that it also plays a role while you are the speaker? When you are speaking, always pay attention to your audience's reactions. You may need to convey some bad news or a new project to a colleague, so it is important that you gauge their response and understanding of the topic.

Nonverbal cues such as body language, posture, and facial expressions will immediately tell you how your listener is interpreting your message, and if you need to adapt or further explain it.

Be Friendly

Demonstrating that you are friendly and sympathetic makes a bad situation easier to handle. Use phrases such as "I will do what I can to help" to help convey your sympathy towards the other person.

Be Prepared

Anticipate possible responses to your message and have answers to those issues prepared. In this way, if someone challenges you with a negative "But what about…" scenario, you can have a solution in place. If you do not know the answer or cannot help them yourself, direct the audience to someone who can. This will build credibility for you and increases their likelihood to trust you.

Be Clear and Concise

When a speaker takes a long time to get to the point, the result is wasted time and an increased risk of misunderstandings. Watch the pace of your message: speaking too fast or too slow can reduce the clarity of the topic. If a message is too fast, your audience may feel rushed and anxious. However, if a message is too slow, your audience may feel bored, and will lose interest. Be sure to get to the point as soon as you can while still adequately explaining the situation.

Watch your audience—their body language will tell you how they are receiving your message and if you need to adjust your pace. Check in periodically by asking if they have any questions. Summarize at the end of the communication what was decided, and ensure your audience agrees.

Be Yourself

In a conversation, do not try to be someone you are not. The general population is adept at knowing if someone is not genuine. Being dishonest during a conversation makes you come across as disingenuous and disrespectful to the other person. It will undermine your credibility.

Not Always About You

Understand that not every single conversation is completely about you and there are always other parties involved. You might be feeling sorry for yourself if there are cutbacks at work, and while that is a legitimate feeling, keep in mind that the company might be experiencing financial difficulties due to outside factors. When discussing this situation with someone, such as a co-worker or supervisor, be prepared to ask questions:

- What can I do to change the situation?
- When do we expect the situation to change?
- How is the situation impacting others?
- What external forces created the situation?
- Are we in control of these forces?
- When do you anticipate this situation will end?

Asking questions helps you gain perspective.

5.3: Effective Speaking Techniques

One requires effective delivery techniques in a number of situations:

- A major presentation
- Delivering information at a staff meeting
- Working with clients
- Job interviews
- Interviews for promotions

Effective speaking techniques increase your self-confidence, self-image, credibility, and can further your career. Practise the following techniques to improve your speaking skills.

Know Your Audience

Understanding your audience is key to effective communication, regardless of whether it is a formal presentation, an interview, or a meeting with staff or clients. For example, you want to speak differently to a trusted friend than how you would during a business meeting with management at work.

Knowing your audience helps determine elements such as the tone of voice, the type of language, the type of information that they might find more important, and the level of detail they will require. Understanding these elements allows you to tailor the communication to your specific audience.

The Three Cs

In order to be an effective public speaker, practise being clear, concise, and consistent every time you speak.

- **Clear Speech:** Common pitfalls are mumbling your words or speaking too quickly or slowly.
    - Doing so can interfere with the clarity of your words and reduce the listener's comprehension of your overall point.
    - Enunciate so each listener can hear each word and phrase clearly.
    - Project your voice so everyone in the room is able to hear you.
    - We often speak quickly or too softly when we are nervous. Be aware of your voice and speech at all times.

- **Concise:** The main goal of any conversation is to ensure the listener understands the intended point. Always be concise when you speak.
    - If you are longwinded and overly wordy, you can lose your point, leaving the listener confused.
    - However, do not be too brief. Ensure you include the entire message so you do not leave your audience asking questions because your message was incomplete.

- **Consistent:** When you are speaking to multiple people about the same topic, particularly when the conversations or meetings are separate, ensure that your message remains consistent.
    - Do not change your story or presentation to have a different core message for different people. It can get confusing if members of your audiences converse with one another and discover that they heard conflicting stories.

Practise, Practise, Practise

Whenever you have a presentation or upcoming meeting, always make sure that you have a good plan in place. Try writing a script for your presentation, even if you just use some detailed bullet points. Practise it multiple times before the main event.

Practising a speech or presentation helps commit your words to long-term memory. This helps your presentation come naturally.

Move Past Mistakes

If you make a mistake when you are speaking, take a breath and continue. If it was a significant mistake, you can and should correct yourself, but you are often the only one who will notice your smaller mistakes. Drawing attention to them can take away from your point, reduces your credibility, or confuses your audience. Do not acknowledge it. Simply move on.

Discussion

Promoting a discussion at the end of any meeting and presentation greatly increases the effectiveness of your oral communication skills. It provides your audience with the opportunity to ask questions to get more detail on the topic or project. This can increase your audience's understanding of the presentation's intended message.

Decide when would be the most appropriate time for discussion. If your topic and size of audience and venue permits, allow discussion to take place during the presentation. Generate discussion by allowing an open forum or question and answer period at the end of the presentation.

Do Your Research

It is critical to prepare for every presentation, including client or staff meetings. This includes any required research, such as a brief client history, information on products or services, or a detailed plan and background on a proposed project.

Doing your research increases your credibility in presenting solid facts. It also prepares you with additional information for questions that may arise during the presentation or meeting.

5.4: Nonverbal Communication

When people first think about oral communication skills, they tend to focus on speaking. However, nonverbal communication adds another layer to public speaking. **Nonverbal communication** involves the display and understanding of wordless cues, such as body language, eye contact, posture, gestures, as well as tone of voice and word choice, which individuals and groups of people may interpret differently. The meaning and intention behind your words might be innocent, but if your nonverbal communication conflicts with your verbal message, your message might be misunderstood.

Nonverbal communication sends a signal—try to make it a good one!

Types of Nonverbal Communication

Nonverbal communication comprises a large range of behaviours that occur while we are communicating. There are a number of different types of nonverbal communication that work together to effectively enhance your verbal communication.

Body Language

Gestures

Our body plays an important physical role in all of our conversations. For example, our hands could gesture to indicate how large something was, or convey sympathy by softly touching a friend's shoulder. Fidgeting with your hands, feet, and hair can convey disinterest, even if you do not intend it. Tapping a pen can indicate irritation or impatience.

Someone who is speaking angrily may speed up their hand motions, intensifying their point. Also, angry gestures such as pointing or thrusting a pen can intimidate an audience and cause defensiveness. This will impede your message's effectiveness.

However, if used properly, hand gestures can display confidence and passion to your listeners. They can help lead your audience towards a point, while inviting them to participate in a conversation.

Facial Expressions

If you use an angry facial expression when informing your audience about good news your body language will send a different message than what you say. When you are speaking or listening, try to control the expression on your face to match the verbal message. If you are telling someone that they are receiving a promotion, a smile on your face extends the message of happiness for their success.

What message is this expression sending?

If you do not want to give your opinion away when you are listening, keep your face in a friendly, but neutral, expression. This ensures that while you are keeping things to yourself, the person speaking to you is not offended or misinterpreting your expression as negative.

Try to keep your face neutral when you have to deliver negative news. A happy face could be interpreted as you taking joy in someone else's misfortune, even though you intend for it to cheer them up and not make the situation seem so bad.

Be aware of your own facial expressions at different times, such as when you are tired or in contemplation. If you are not sure of how someone is feeling, such as if you are seeing conflicting body or facial expressions, check in by asking, "Is everything fine?" to help your audience feel comfortable.

Facial expressions have an impact over the phone as well. When on the phone, smile when you are speaking. This helps adjust your tone to not to sound abrasive or harsh.

Eye Contact

Making eye contact indicates friendliness and approachability in many Western cultures. Avoiding eye contact indicates that you might be closed off to their attention or do not wish to talk. However, too much eye contact or staring can be intimidating, making the person you are looking at feel uncomfortable. Try to strike a balance between the two extremes.

Keep in mind, however, that different cultures interpret eye contact differently. Some consider looking someone directly in the eye a sign of disrespect, whereas shifting your gaze away is respectful. Be aware of the cultures you are working with to avoid misunderstandings.

This person seems scared.
Would you agree?

Body Position

The position of your body before you start talking to someone can be very telling. A closed body position, such as crossed arms and turning your torso away from a person, can indicate hostility and that you may not be receptive to their message. Sitting with your body directed towards the person who is talking along with unfolded arms can show friendliness and an open mind. A slouched posture, much like crossed arms and turning your torso away, may indicate disinterest and disrespect to a speaker.

Paralinguistics

Paralinguistics involves vocal signals that go beyond the basic verbal message. This involves the tone, rate, and volume of verbal speech. Look at the following sentence:

> Tomorrow morning there will be an important meeting
> in the boardroom at 11am.

What would your first thought be if your boss said that in a monotone or subdued tone of voice? Chances are you would imagine that they were going to deliver bad news, and if you found out that the company just obtained a high-value client, you might feel confused.

If someone is speaking loudly, others assume they are angry, even if that person is neutral or that is their normal level of speaking. As well, someone talking very fast may come off as anxious or potentially disinterested in the conversation.

Adding vocal inflections and tone helps enhance presentations by showing the listeners your passion and interest in the topic, as well as your opinions and mood. If you display passion and interest in your topic, the chances that your audience will actively engage in the topic increase.

Think about any presentation you have seen in the past. Was it effective or not? If not, can you identify why? What would have made it a better presentation?

Hint: To see how you look and speak, record yourself giving a presentation. You will be surprised at the unconscious verbal and nonverbal ticks that can happen when you speak of which you were not aware, and that no one ever mentioned to you.

Personal Space

What would you think if someone you did not know very well—such as a stranger on the bus—sat very close to you? Most people would feel uncomfortable and as if this stranger invaded their personal space. That uncomfortable feeling often translates to a negative opinion of that person.

Personal space is an important element of nonverbal communication in business. The amount of personal space that an individual needs varies based on their gender, culture, and relationship with the other person. In general, the closer their relationship, the less space they need to be comfortable.

In a business setting, you can likely be closer to your colleagues than you would with a stranger and still feel comfortable. However, keep in mind that because it is a business setting, a professional distance between people is still required. This is why invading someone's personal space is seen as aggressive and unprofessional.

Appearance

First impressions make all the difference. Before you speak, everyone around you is getting a nonverbal impression. Your appearance factors into this.

Be aware of the corporate culture of the company you are working with. Is the corporate culture very formal (such a bank or brokerage house), or is it more relaxed and informal (such as a software firm)? In the following scenario, imagine that you are interviewing candidates for an entry-level position in your marketing company.

The Candidates		
Candidate 1	**Candidate 2**	**Candidate 3**
• Comes to the interview wearing a ripped pair of baggy jeans • Plain white t-shirt with mustard stains • Sneakers • Gold necklace	• Wearing jeans • Navy blue golf shirt • Worn sneakers • Subtle pendant necklace	• Pressed grey dress pants • Dark purple dress shirt, buttoned, with a plain white t-shirt underneath • Black dress shoes • No jewellery

Even before each candidate begins to speak and answer your questions, you are already forming an opinion about each of them. What are they projecting to you about the kind of person they are and their interest in the advertised position?

If you were not able to speak to any of them, based on your initial impression, which of the three candidates do you think you are most likely going to hire? Businesses have different corporate cultures and as a result, the accepted level of dress may vary. When being interviewed, the general accepted practice is to dress a step above the dress code of the office.

When interviewing for a new job, make sure that your diction, language, and body language are coordinated with your dress code. Even if you are professionally dressed, chewing gum, swearing, and behaving in a rude manner may cost you the job.

Exercise

What have you worn to interviews in the past?

....

....

....

....

....

....

....

....

....

What will you wear to your next interview?

....

....

....

....

....

....

....

....

....

....

....

Tips to Improve Nonverbal Communication

Emotional Awareness and Management

One of the most important factors in nonverbal communication is emotion. Unfortunately, it is also the most volatile and can severely compromise the message that you are sending if it gets out of control.

The first tip to improving your nonverbal communication skills is learning how to manage your emotions, especially in a business setting. This is especially important when you are passionate about your presentation's topic. Let's put it into perspective with a potential scenario.

Most large companies have corporate social responsibility practices, such as donating to local or international charities. Often employees selected to make pitches for charities choose causes close to their hearts. Showing passion towards the charity is beneficial; however, you should still manage your personal emotions about the cause.

This goes beyond showing professionalism during your presentation. With this type of business situation, there is sure to be a question period where people share criticisms. If you do not manage your emotions, you may lose control and become irritated about these criticisms, indicating unprofessionalism to your audience.

Remember to focus on the message rather than the person when responding to criticism. When offering feedback to an individual, frame your message in a way that focuses on quantifiable facts, not on subjective or personal feelings.

For example, if your co-worker is passionate about a group supporting war- or weather-ravaged regions, commend their awareness. However, when declining their request, include facts such as:

We were not aware of this group and the outstanding work that they do. However, we already support XYZ organisation, which does similar work in the region. We are not looking to support other organizations at this time.

Watch for Inconsistencies

Nonverbal communication signals should act as a reinforcement to what people say during a conversation or presentation. However, sometimes you find that people send conflicting signals.

They may be giving a positive verbal response, but are shaking their head while doing so. They could be delivering bad news, but be smiling. Pay attention to any inconsistencies that you see. Oftentimes the nonverbal signals indicate the person's true feelings on a particular subject. This is because there is a higher likelihood that nonverbal signals are unconscious.

Eye Contact

Keep a balance between no eye contact and constant eye contact when you are speaking. In a group setting, shift your eyes from person to person. If you are giving a presentation to five clients about a new potential investment opportunity, move your eyes from the first client to the second, then to the third, and so on.

Feel free to change the order as the presentation goes forward, but look at each of the clients equally so that it does not look as if you are favouring anyone. Changing the individual with whom you are making eye contact minimizes the risk of unnerving someone through constant eye contact (staring). Use your peripheral vision to watch for responses around the room.

If you are in a one-on-one setting, you cannot maintain eye contact with your listener the entire time or you will unnerve them with your staring. Make eye contact for the majority of the time you are speaking, but periodically look elsewhere, such as back at your presentation slides or other materials but in a way that enhances your point. When answering a person, look at them while you are speaking.

Monitor Expression

Whether you are speaking or listening, you should keep a close watch on the other person's expression. This will give you some insight on what they might be thinking or how they are feeling. Once you have this insight, you can adapt your presentation or listening expression as needed to meet their expectations or help to sway their opinion.

If you are in a group, do not overthink individual nonverbal signals. Instead, take in an overview and evaluate the majority of the signals, from facial expressions and gestures to tone of voice and overall body language. Once you have done that you can examine their overall consistency.

Watch Posture

Slouching in your chair gives off an air of disrespect, as well as an overall dismissive and unprofessional impression to the speaker. So, while you are listening, be sure to watch your posture and sit up straight in your chair. You can choose to have your legs crossed or uncrossed based on your taste and comfort.

However, leaning away when you cross your legs indicates closed body language. Instead, when you cross your legs lean slightly towards the other person. Sitting properly in your chair automatically signals that you are interested, professional, and are paying attention to the speaker.

Train at Home

When trying to improve your nonverbal communication skills, practise is very important. A safe way to practise proper posture, is to sit down in a chair in front of a mirror in the comfort of your own home.

Practise every presentation multiple times. Doing so will not only allow you to remember what you have to say and sound more natural during the presentation, but will also provide you with time to practise hand gestures and facial expressions.

Practise until you are very familiar with the content. Do not try for straight memorization alone. If your presentation is interrupted for any reason, you could be at risk for forgetting some of it.

Know your presentation well enough so you are able to deliver your core message, even in a worst-case scenario. When you are familiar with what you have to say, you can afford to shift some attention to the nonverbal signals you should use during the presentation.

Think About Context

Inappropriate nonverbal communication, even when unintentional, can have a significant negative effect on how others perceive you. Before you decide what type of nonverbal communication you should engage in, think about the context.

For example, formal business situations require nonverbal signals that people often interpret differently in informal scenarios. You want to sit straight with your legs crossed in a formal business meeting with management, however, you can adopt a more casual posture (leaning forward and having uncrossed legs) when speaking in a team meeting with your co-workers.

Just Relax

Trying to remember all of the little tricks involving nonverbal communication can become overwhelming. Try to relax, while keeping in mind how posture and eye contact alter your professional image.

Being too stiff in a presentation because you are trying to focus on every tiny detail of your performance can be just as detrimental as negative nonverbal signals. Remember to take a moment and take a deep breath to calm yourself. You are often your own harshest critic.

my notes

....

....

....

....

....

....

....

....

....

....

....

....

5.5: Intercultural Communication

In addition to verbal and nonverbal communication, there is also intercultural communication to consider, which happens when people share information across different cultures. You must have a thorough understanding of different cultures and how intercultural communication works, because the signals that you are familiar with could have a different meaning, or none at all, to people from another region.

An accent can influence pronunciation and may have an impact on how well you are understood. The most basic tip—and the most important—is to practise when learning to speak a new language. Ask for advice on pronunciation and word choice. Most people are more than willing to help.

Pronunciation and Enunciation
When learning a new language, over-pronounce and take care to enunciate each of your words. While it may feel silly and unnatural, it can often make it seem like you are progressing further in a shorter space of time. Additionally, when you are just beginning to learn the language, over pronouncing the words can often have the same effect as trying to pronounce them normally later on in the process.

When attempting to pronounce the words, work with phonetics. If in doubt, use what you already know about the accent and pronounce the words how you think they would sound phonetically. Many online dictionaries and translators offer this service.

Slow Down

Too many non-native speakers make the mistake of trying to talk at the same speed as fluent native speakers simply to keep up with them. In many cases, their thought is that if they talk at the same pace, they will gain more respect and will not be looked down on.

Unfortunately, trying to speak a new language at the same speed as native speakers can often have a negative effect if you are harder to understand. With this in mind, slow down when you are presenting, and take your time to pronounce each word correctly and clearly.

Translation

When you are communicating between different cultures, one of the first issues that can arise is a language barrier. When you have two different languages, there are often expressions that you cannot translate in the literal sense because their intended meaning would be lost. If the intended meaning is lost, the potential for offense increases.

Instead, when engaging in intercultural communication where translation is involved, use the intended overall feeling and message that you wish to get across rather than literal translations of each individual word. Consider employing a professional translator to make these situations easier to navigate.

Slang Words

Related to translation: each language has its own slang. As previously detailed in this textbook, slang refers to words and other phrases considered informal and region or culture-specific. Trying to use the same slang in different regions with the same language can be incredibly difficult, even without trying to traverse cultures with different languages. In business, avoid using slang and use formal language to remain professional and alleviate any translation issues.

Body Language in Culture

Communicating between people of the same culture can sometimes be difficult when people do not consider or use elements such as body language appropriately. This is also the case with intercultural communication. Be aware how other cultures observe body language, personal space, and touching. A misstep with any of these can cause miscommunications.

Different Nonverbal Meanings

Many people believe that the gestures made in business presentations, meetings, and general conversations are universal. This means that they do not change regardless of who or where you are. However, different cultures can assign different meanings to nonverbal signals.

For example, a typical greeting may be kissing each other on the cheek instead of shaking hands. As well, other nations may consider common North American gestures offensive, such as men shaking hands with women in certain Muslim cultures. This is why you should never assume that nonverbal communication is universal. Make an effort to understand the customs of the cultures with which you are working.

Sample of Differences Between Cultures

Canada/United States/etc.	Some Asian Cultures
Gesturing for a person to come towards you with your palm facing up and moving your fingers towards you (one or even more).	Some cultures in Asia believe the "come here" gesture, though common in North America, is very rude. Instead, the opposite motion (palm downwards and moving fingers back and forth—like in Canada you are telling someone to leave) is the appropriate gesture.

If you know that you are going to encounter other cultures in the workplace, whether it is through a business trip or video conference, there are certain factors that merit consideration. Practicing professional intercultural communication skills comprises three parts: attitude, knowledge, and skill.

Positive Attitude
A negative or aggressive demeanour may indicate to your foreign visitor that you are not to be trusted or that you are rude. This can result in them being offended, which can compromise business deals. Demonstrating that you have a positive attitude can go a long way when you interact with foreign business partners. They may understand that you are attempting to be friendly and professional even if you do not get everything right.

Knowledge
Studying any foreign culture that you will encounter during business interactions can greatly improve your intercultural communication, and at least should prevent any serious incidents.

You can be unintentionally rude if you do not attempt to understand other cultures. Take some time out of your day to prepare for an upcoming foreign business meeting and understand what the normal cultural practices are for the other parties involved. They may attempt to understand your culture, but you cannot always rely on your audience's understanding.

Additionally, they may not understand everything correctly and will revert to what they know. If you have an approximate understanding of what they are trying to say or show you, the chances of miscommunication reduce significantly.

Additional Skill

Developing skill in interacting with different cultures reduces the likelihood of translation and communication problems in international business settings. Skill only comes with knowledge and practise surrounding a certain topic or culture. Beyond doing basic research, here are some strategies that you can use to improve your intercultural communication skills.

Teach Each Other

When you have an international business contact, consider proposing that all parties try to teach each other about their cultural norms. Start by making a list of the most important things that you would want others to know about your culture, and then ask yourself what you would want to understand about the other culture. Ask your associates to do the same.

Allocate some time at the beginning of your meeting to go over each list, understanding that at this point the entire purpose is to learn and develop your skills. This means that no one should expect the other to be fully versed in his or her cultural practices at the beginning.

Simulated Situations

Within your own company, take the group of people who will be interacting with other cultures and create some situations that may come up in your international business encounter, such as who pays for a business dinner.

Consider what you would do in your native culture before researching what the foreign culture expects in this situation. Once you have that knowledge, develop your skills by running the scenario over again, but practice the foreign culture's expected actions this time.

5.6: Positive Versus Negative Communication

Positive Communication

Effective communication ensures that the intended message accurately transfers to another person. If it is ineffective, others may misinterpret the message and the point is lost.

It is also important to practise positive communication techniques. Positive communication in a business environment helps to solidify respectful working relationships, improve employee morale, increase business efficiency, and promote overall positive attitudes. Below are some of the most popular and effective positive communication practices that employees can use at all levels of the company.

Open Door Policy

Every manager and project leader should make themselves available to all employees involved in their department, during working hours. This is known as an open door policy, where the manager makes it known to employees that they are able to come in with questions about work issues.

This may mean asking for clarification about an aspect of the project they are currently working on, or even for some updates regarding other employees. Regardless of the specific issue, a manager needs to make it clear that they are open to communication.

Constructive Feedback

Giving feedback on someone's work is crucial in any business environment. However, in many cases people do not follow positive communication practises and a large number of employees are receiving feedback such as "this report is weak and needs to be improved," before they are handed back their project to make the necessary changes. Unfortunately, this does not help the employee if they do not know what to focus on.

Constructive feedback makes sure that the employee is completely aware of what has happened and what they need to do. The feedback is always comprised of what is positive and what needs improvement. If a person only gives out one or the other, the receiver will eventually distrust and disregard what they are told.

In addition to providing specificity in feedback, put some focus on descriptions rather than black or white judgements or observations. Finally, only highlight two or three specific points at one time to avoid an overload of feedback.

Respect

Whether you are delivering good or bad news, ensure that you do so respectfully. This usually involves implementing practices like active listening and constructive feedback.

When an individual knows that people respect them, they are much more likely to continue a friendly working relationship with the other person. Additionally, an employee is more likely to continue to respect their boss or manager if they feel respected.

In Person Connections

Communicating through email is the most convenient option available in the modern business environment. However, it should not be the exclusive form of communication. To maximize positive communication techniques, make a point of adding phone and face-to-face conversations to business routines.

Take the time to walk across the office for a conversation about a new project, or pick up the phone to arrange a meeting if you are in a large company where walking across the office is not an option. Doing so helps demonstrate commitment and respect to those around the office.

Negative Communication

Negative communication is the result of failing to express our personal feelings, in addition to ignoring the feelings of others. It also includes a disrespectful attitude and failing to communciate the intended message to business colleagues.

However, what is it that makes negative communication so impactful? Below are a couple of issues that result from negative communication. They can have detrimental effects on any business environment. In order to avoid as many of these issues as possible, keep in mind all of the techniques this chapter has already discussed regarding postive communications.

Conflicts and Arguments

Unclear messages and misinterpreted meanings can often be the beginning of conflicts and arguments in the workplace. An employee may believe that someone has disrespected them and that the other person (or group) is being excessively rude. If they believe this, the employee may begin to display rudeness and disrespect to the others involved.

Additionally, if a manager's assistant relayed instructions without adequate details, the receiving employee may express anger and overall resentment towards the assistant and the manager, even if the incomplete instructions were unintentional. This would foster a conflict, even though one party may remain unaware of exactly why it started in the first place. Remember to speak clearly and in a concise manner to avoid contributing to conflicts.

Low Employee Morale

If employees are not receiving the necessary information and messages are constantly misinterpreted, they may need to repeat their work. When this happens, there is a reduction in the employees' motivation to continue putting in one hundred percent.

If morale and motivation are low, employees reduce the company's overall productivity. Jobs are in jeopardy if productivity is low. Employees will not feel valued at this time, and morale will suffer. All staff should feel that they can communicate ideas to help improve a situation and feel empowered to do their jobs.

Bias

Bias is the inclination to feel or show prejudice against a person, place, or object, or favour towards another. It is only human nature to experience some kind of bias or prejudice at certain times.

Bias in the workplace may start small with seemingly miniscule results, but can quickly turn catastrophic. While eliminating bias is quite difficult, simply acknowledging that you are experiencing it can help steer the situation in the right direction.

Fact and Fiction

In business, you can also view the difference between positive and negative communication as the separation of fact from fiction. When communicating in a business setting, it is important to differentiate the facts of the conversation or meeting from any misinformation or 'fiction' that you may hear if someone else is not trying to communicate effectively with you.

Chapter 5 Recap

As we close this chapter, let's review the concepts, skills, and key takeaway points that we covered throughout this chapter.

- Engaging in active listening means paying close attention to the speaker, without distractions, and crafting a professional response after they have finished.

- Verbal etiquette is more than just being polite: it means you pay attention to your audience, remain clear, concise, and objective when dealing with business scenarios.

- Effective public speaking techniques include clear, concise, and consistent speech. Practise a detailed understanding of your audience, research, discussion, and a calm demeanour to avoid any potential mistakes.

- Nonverbal communication signals including body language, gestures, appearances, and paralinguistics add an additional layer to business interactions.

- Improving nonverbal communication means a heightened awareness and management of emotions, detection of inconsistencies between verbal and nonverbal signals, training, taking into account the context of the situation, and simple relaxation.

- Communicating across different cultures requires understanding cultural differences, including how certain actions translate differently, and how to consider these with understanding and cooperation.

- Positive communication—respect, constructive feedback, and an open door policy—holds immeasurable benefits, whereas failing to respond professionally has devastating effects, including low morale, bias, and conflicts.

Chapter 5 Quiz

1. Which of the following is a component of active listening?

    a. Interrupting the speaker
    b. Texting while they are talking
    c. Providing constructive feedback to the speaker
    d. Looking over their shoulder

2. In active listening, you should summarize, respond, and ask open-ended questions.

    a. True
    b. False

3. What does active listening demonstrate to the speaker?

    a. Engagement with the topic
    b. Respect
    c. Understanding of the issue at hand
    d. All of the above

4. Which of the following is not an element of verbal etiquette:

    a. Clear and Concise
    b. Slouching Body Posture
    c. Be Friendly
    d. Listen While Speaking

5. Speaking immediately can mean rash actions, so you should always:

    a. Trust your instinct
    b. Evaluate how to fix the situation afterwards
    c. Do not speak at all
    d. Think before you speak

6. Doing research, moving beyond mistakes, and practising are all components of:

    a. Effective speaking techniques
    b. Nonverbal communication
    c. Intercultural communication
    d. Active listening

7. Body language is composed of body position, eye movements, gestures, and:

    a. Tone of voice
    b. Facial expressions
    c. Physical appearance
    d. Verbal speech

8. Personal space is not a component of nonverbal communication.

    a. True
    b. False

9. To improve your nonverbal communication skills, you should:

    a. Manage your emotions
    b. Make eye contact
    c. Relax
    d. A and B
    e. All of the above

10. Practising professional intercultural communication skills is comprised of three parts. Those three parts are:

    a. Attitude, knowledge, power
    b. Knowledge, skill, practice
    c. Attitude, knowledge, skill
    d. Skill, perseverance, attitude

11. To enhance your intercultural communication skill, you should:

    a. Simulate situations
    b. Teach each other
    c. A and B
    d. None of the above

12. Which of the following is not a component of selective listening listed in this chapter:

    a. Summarizing
    b. Multitasking
    c. Filtering
    d. All of them are components

Answers:

....
....
....
....
....
....
....
....
....
....
....
....
....
....
....
....
....
....
....
....
....
....

Meetings and Presentations

Despite the fact that many people in business consider themselves effective communicators, oral communication in a professional environment can be very difficult. Good oral communication skills are necessary in business in order to use time and money efficiently. They also help you avoid any detrimental consequences in company dealings. Let's build on those skills discussed in Chapter 5: *Developing Oral Communication Skills*.

Although it may be convenient, do not limit oral communication to Monday morning or Friday afternoon staff meetings. While these meetings are a good starting point, limiting communications with employees and colleagues to these times restricts the potential, clarity, and friendliness of the workplace.

Presentations take a number of forms in the workplace. These can include team meetings, meetings with management, and presentations to existing or new clients. Presentations can be effective in communicating ideas and projects. Business presentations require a high degree of planning in order to be as effective as possible. This chapter contains sections that review techniques and elements of effective presentations.

Learning Goals

- Understand poor team dynamics, the problems they cause, and how to improve them.
- Identify the elements of a successful business meeting and other beneficial tips.
- Understand the damage caused by misunderstanding a colleague or supervisor.
- Learn different presentation techniques, how to apply them, and their effects on your audience.
- Understand the importance of practising before the presentation.
- Understand the importance of the proper use of visuals.
- Understand how to create an effective PowerPoint presentation.
- Learn how to deal with stage fright.

my notes

6.1: Business Meetings

A business meeting is an example of a setting in which communication skills are critical. Meetings allow team members to come together to brainstorm, resolve issues, and plan future projects. Unfortunately, business meetings are often ineffective as they run longer than expected and have a lack of direction and resolutions. This results in the perception that the meeting was a waste of time.

Often, business leaders do not plan meetings well, resulting in unprepared attendees who are unsure about the purpose of the meeting. The following strategies help create more effective and productive meetings:

Preparation Is Key

Preparation is key for a successful meeting. A meeting will be successful if the meeting leader and the meeting participants have a common purpose and defined goals, provided they work towards those goals. Steps to prepare include:

- **Timing:** What time will the meeting start? What time will it end?
    - Make a schedule for the meeting, outlining the amount of time you can take.
    - Limit meetings to 45 minutes or less. Employees have other responsibilities.

- **Place:** Every meeting needs a location, regardless of what specific type it is.
    - Ensure that the location is an appropriate size, so all attendees are comfortable.
    - Invite the appropriate attendees, and inform all attendees of the location. Provide a dial-in number if this is a conference call.

- **Agenda:** No meeting is complete without an accompanying agenda.
    - A quality agenda includes a list of the attendees, a meeting time and location, and a chart of all the topics the meeting will cover.
    - The agenda will include details such as who will be presenting, the time that each will take, and any important points about each topic.
    - An agenda helps keep everyone on topic throughout the meeting.

Exercise

Imagine you are leading a business meeting for your group. It is the first meeting that you are holding for the new project and you need the following things for the complete project: a portfolio including pictures of the product, product description, marketing plan, financial information, and anything else your team deems relevant. What would your meeting agenda look like?

my notes

During the Meeting

- **Participation:** When you are conducting the meeting, ensure you keep people engaged. This might be through a game, questions, ideas, or other general comments.
  - The specific tactics will vary based on the type of meeting being held.
  - Allow each attendee to discuss something so that no one person or group dominates the discussion.
  - The most effective meetings are when everyone has the chance to discuss their ideas.

- **Action items:** Informing employees about company updates is important. However, it may not necessarily require a staff meeting—an email may suffice.
  - Meetings, in order to increase their effectiveness, are best when composed of action items. This is where individuals and groups have a specific task to complete, instead of a vague idea with no distinct plan.

- **Listen:** A mistake that many make during meetings is failing to listen properly.
  - Perhaps they are distracted, though this is generally simple to rectify if meetings do not permit technology apart from what is necessary.
  - Many also listen with the intent to reply, rather than to understand the message that the speaker is trying to communicate.

- **Include:** All relevant information, and provide it to the attendees.

As the meeting leader, let attendees know what the meeting is about, and why you invited them to the meeting. If you want people to present materials or ideas, notify them so they know what they will be doing and can therefore plan what they will say. A well-organized leader will execute an effective business meeting.

Other Tips

- **Fewer Meetings:** Frequent meetings can actually be counterproductive to an ongoing project or the overall productivity of a company.
    - If there are no important updates regarding the project or a company product, or no specific purpose with other new information, the meeting time is wasted. Cancel it and set up a recurring meeting every 2 weeks, 2 months, or the best span of time for the department.
    - Ensure you keep the topic of each meeting focused. This increases each meeting's overall productivity.

- **Pre-Meetings:** If there will be more than one presenter during a meeting, consider having what some may term a "pre-meeting" and get together with the presenters.
    - This will help everyone to plan the meeting and its transitions, so that everything runs smoothly.
    - Each presenter will know exactly what they need to do and how much time they have.

my notes

....
....
....
....
....
....
....
....
....
....
....
....
....
....

6.2: Team Dynamics

Teams are a cornerstone of the modern workplace: this leads to the topic of team dynamics. The goal is to ensure that the team works to its full potential. A team is a specific instance of a group with a shared goal. The members are all dependent on one another in order to be successful, like a sports team.

Problematic Team Dynamics

The first step in finding a solution for any issue is to identify problematic elements. How can you fix something if you do not know exactly what is wrong? In this section, we will identify the major categories of problematic team dynamics.

Conflict: An argument between two or more individuals. Conflict within a team decreases productivity, especially when there is an unwillingness to see the other points of view.

Scapegoating: When someone is blamed for the faults or wrongdoings of others. This is a common source of conflict within teams.

Non-participation: When one or more people are not participating in problem solving or team discussions. For example, a person's ideas may not have received appropriate discussion time, their attempts to participate were ignored, or the group only gave them a limited time to speak. In any case, this is another common team dynamic issue.

Monopolization: This typically involves one person taking exclusive control over the meeting and agenda, often forcing their own agenda on the team.

Refusing to participate means nothing gets done!

Causes of Poor Team Dynamics

So what exactly causes these poor team dynamics? Both the team leader and team members can contribute to the negative dynamic, so it is essential to recognize the symptoms before situations, like the examples detailed above, arise within the team.

Weak Leadership

One of the major causes of poor group dynamics is weak leadership. If the team itself lacks a strong leader, another member of the team with a dominant personality may take over and monopolize the team's actions and other efforts.

If this happens, the team may lack a clear and defined direction, focus on the wrong issues, or have any number of other conflicts if the dominant personality consistently pushes the chosen leader to the side.

"Yes Man" Syndrome

Another cause of poor team dynamics results from one or more members of the team constantly agreeing with the leader without any discussion (holding back their opinions). Such members are trying to make others see them as cooperative and very agreeable.

Blocking

Another common behaviour of individual team members is "blocking" the discussion and transmission of information. This includes withdrawing from discussion and refusing to contribute ideas, constantly criticizing other people's ideas, expressing inappropriate humour, and always seeking recognition.

Groupthink

Be aware of the phenomenon known as **groupthink**. This is when all members of the team place a higher value on reaching a consensus (where every member of the team agrees) rather than focusing on coming to the right decision in a particular situation. It often means that the group does not make the best possible decision, as everyone is focused on agreeing rather than offering differing opinions and discussing them.

Good Team Dynamics

This section will detail the ideal team dynamics that each team should strive to achieve and maintain.

Effective Leader Behaviours

Upon establishing the team, the group, inclusive of all members, must select an appropriate leader based upon skill, as well as their willingness to take on a leadership role. A good leader ensures the team remains effective throughout the project. They also facilitate problem-solving, report to required outside parties (such as company management), and raise issues beyond the scope of the group, if necessary.

Member Roles and Responsibilities

Discuss the roles and attached responsibilities that the team requires for the project. With the leader acting as the facilitator in these discussions, the team should decide upon roles to enhance the effectiveness of the team's overall capabilities, with each member working to their strengths. Ensure that members are clear on what their responsibilities are to eliminate any confusion or overlap.

Employ Team Building Activities

In some cases, poor dynamics are the result of a team not knowing one another well, potentially reflected as mistrust or personality misunderstandings. To avoid this scenario, the team leader can start the project in the first meeting with one or more team-building activities. This helps to increase comfort levels and trust, in addition to understanding how other members of the team work.

Here are a few team-building activities you can try with your team:

1. Drawing in Pairs

a. Split your team into groups of two. One person should have a piece of paper and a pencil. The other person should have a picture of a shape.

b. Without actually naming the shape, the person with the picture provides instructions to the other, who will attempt to draw the shape.

c. Afterwards, compare the drawing with the picture and evaluate the process.
- Were the instructions unclear?
- How could they improve?
- Did the drawer interpret the instructions correctly?

d. Have each pair switch roles, this time drawing a new shape.

2. Minefield/Obstacle Course

a. Prepare a large area with obstacles such as chairs, plants, et cetera.

b. Split your team into pairs. Blindfold one person in each pair.

c. The blindfolded individual walks through the minefield trying to avoid the obstacles based on the instructions of their partner, who will stand outside of the minefield.

   • You can allow a few minutes at the beginning for each pair to determine how they will communicate to one another.

3. Lower to the Ground

a. Have the team split into two equal lines facing each other.

b. Have everyone hold out their hands and make a fist, except for their index fingers.

c. Rest one long stick or rod on their index fingers of each person.

d. The goal is to lower the stick all the way to the ground as one whole team.

e. Their fingers must always touch the stick, and they cannot pinch or otherwise hold the stick (it has to rest on top of their fingers).

Exercise

Create your own team-building exercise, taking inspiration from the examples in the textbook.

Clarity of Purpose and Preparation for the Meeting

Misinterpretations, conflict, and other poor team dynamics are often the result of a lack of communication clarity or preparation. Initial instructions for a project must clearly outline everything that is required, including all pertinent information (such as length of a document, special considerations, et cetera). Incomplete or otherwise unclear instructions make conflicts much more likely in a team setting. Carefully review instructions before sending them out.

As noted previously in this chapter, having an agenda in every meeting demonstrates appropriate preparation. Without adequate planning, meetings can often run overtime, and other aspects of the project become inefficient, costing valuable time and money.

Informal Rules of Order

Ensure that every member of the team understands the informal rules of order for the meeting and everyone has a chance to speak up. Ask quiet members questions, and assign tasks to ensure everyone has an equal opportunity to speak. Do not let dominant personalities override quiet ones in the meeting. Watch for body language, which will tell you how everyone is feeling during the meeting.

Managing Timelines

At the beginning of any project, determine what the individual tasks are and who is responsible for completing each one. Estimate how long each task should take and assign due dates. Keep in mind that certain tasks might require other elements before they can start: use that when organizing the timeline.

Have team members regularly check-in regarding their progress so that you can adjust the timeline if necessary. If deadlines are an issue, consider "flex lines," where the first line is set prior to the actual cut-off line. However, make it clear that this does not mean team members can procrastinate on starting the task, or purposely miss the flex line.

Adjust timelines accordingly if there are unavoidable issues impeding the progress of a project.

6.3: Dangers of Misunderstanding

Misunderstanding another individual is a common issue in business environments. There are countless situations in which a misunderstanding between colleagues or between a supervisor and subordinate can occur, including delivering bad news, criticism, project instructions, new employee training, and language barriers, amongst others.

It is likely that you will experience misunderstandings multiple times throughout your professional career. The consequences associated with misunderstandings in business communication can be serious for individuals, as well as detrimental and potentially catastrophic to a company.

Therefore, misunderstandings and conflicts need to be addressed immediately and in-person. A meeting between those involved needs to take place, and follow up needs to occur to ensure that the correct information flows at all times.

Misunderstandings in business mean that the company is not operating at peak efficiency. If someone misinterprets a given set of instructions, they often do not realize it until later. They usually go through what they think the person meant, and partway through the project find out that was not what they were supposed to do. When an individual realizes they may have misunderstood someone, they often attempt to figure out the true meaning on their own before addressing it with the person who gave them the instructions in the first place.

Time spent on trying to figure out the intended meaning, or correcting mistakes already made because of misunderstanding instructions, is time you could have spent on completing the task correctly in the first place.

Going back to fix mistakes made because of a misunderstanding means it takes longer to complete a project or task. It could even take twice as long, if the revision of the project takes the same amount of time to complete as its initial iteration.

Ensure everyone is aware of the deliverables from the beginning. Have regular check-in meetings or calls to ensure projects are progressing correctly and in a timely manner.

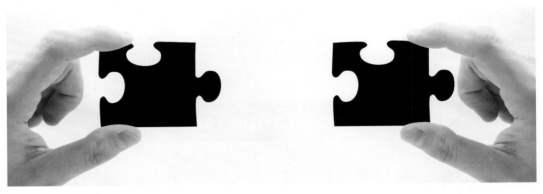

When you misunderstand, you are missing pieces of the puzzle.

my notes

....

....

....

....

....

....

....

....

....

....

....

....

....

6.4: Mechanics of a Presentation

Giving a presentation can be a nerve-wracking experience. At some point throughout their career, almost everyone will put together an oral presentation. A presentation entails speaking in front of other people: co-workers at meetings, job interviews, sales seminars, and so on.

Developing and delivering an effective presentation takes time, planning, and hard work. The following are some presentation planning techniques that can help you simplify the process.

Know Your Audience

Your audience is the most important element to consider in your presentation. Consider their knowledge level about the presentation subject. Will you have to provide lots of detailed information? Do they already have a good knowledge base? What are their hot button words or issues? Can you anticipate any challenges to your points?

Have answers for those ready for the audience. This will make you feel confident, and make you look prepared and professional when you go "live."

Consider what they are expecting to get out of the presentation. This is known as the takeaway. What do you want your audience to know, do, or be able to do, at the end of your presentation?

Your audience will not be a passive group in many cases. During your presentation, address the audience directly, and make regular eye contact with members of your audience. Be prepared for questions and challenges.

The Unsung Hero: Practise

Learning any new skill takes practise, and giving an oral business presentation is no exception. After you finish preparing your presentation, review any notes, slides, or any other material, so they are fresh in your memory.

Run through the presentation multiple times during the days, or hours, before the actual presentation. If there are any issues with words—if you find yourself fumbling or if the wording is too difficult to remember—now is the time to fix these issues. When you are practising, remember to time the whole presentation. You might face limits due to other presentations or just available time for a particular meeting.

Record yourself and play back the recording to see what you are doing well and what you can improve on. However, keep in mind that it is in human nature to speak faster whenever we are nervous. If you are well prepared, you will minimize this effect, but you should still make any necessary accommodations for it.

Exercise

List five things that you will change about your preparation for your next presentation. This can be things you will stop doing or things you will start doing.

With Equipment and Without Equipment

When you are reviewing materials during your practise time, there are some important provisions to make in terms of any multimedia components of your presentation. Multimedia includes PowerPoint, as well as any audio/video clips you intend to use.

Test every piece of multimedia you will be using. You should do this in the actual presentation room with the equipment that will be there during the presentation, as technology can easily malfunction.

However, even if all of your multimedia elements work during your preparation time, keep in mind that technology can still stop working during the actual presentation. Design a presentation that is deliverable without any multimedia and can still get the same message across to the audience. Test websites and ensure they work prior to every presentation.

Going Live

There are many different presentation styles. The least effective style is when the speaker simply reads their slides or notes, not engaging with the audience or adding anything to the message. This presentation style fails to capture your audience's attention.

To avoid this type of presentation, rehearse your presentation materials so that you know them well. Avoid only memorizing your message: if something goes wrong, you may forget everything you know.

Arrive at your presentation venue with enough time to set up, test equipment, and become comfortable with the room and the acoustics. Greet audience members as they arrive. This way, you will see familiar faces in the audience with whom you can connect during the presentation.

Every good presentation has one clear, consistent, and concise message. Presentations with multiple or complicated messages can result in the most important facts being misinterpreted or lost on the audience.

To help keep your presentation clear and concise, break it into sections where appropriate. One component to consider is creating an agenda to hand out or display to your audience. This acts as a roadmap for your presentation, permitting the audience to follow along and understand where you are going with the content.

Including a question and answer period at the end of the presentation is essential to remove any misconceptions and allow clarification on certain points for the audience. Above all, relax as much as professionalism allows during your presentation!

Proper Use of Visuals

Visuals, such as pictues and graphs, can be an effective addition to any presentation. However, you must be careful when choosing to use them. For instance, visuals should simply clarify or enhance your words and not be the basis of your presentation.

This is, in part, because technology can easily malfunction. If your visuals were the entirety of your presentation, you would be unable to present if something went wrong.

Handouts

When working with visuals in a business presentation, consider handing out paper copies of charts or tables. This will give your audience something to refer to afterwards, and, if the technology malfunctions, you can still use the charts as part of your presentation.

Context

Each visual used in a business presentation should have a specific purpose. If there is a picture on a PowerPoint slide, for example, it should connect to the written content on that particular slide.

Additionally, for graphics (such as tables), or other visuals (like videos), refer to them during your presentation. Explain how they connect with the main topic message. Do not simply leave the visual hanging there without context. When using charts or tables in a presentation, ensure that they are simple and easy to read.

Written Visuals

The written content of your slides is equally important. You want to use the correct font style and font size. In the case of font style, choose a simple font for readability, such as Times New Roman, instead of something fancy.

Part of the presentation is lost if the audience cannot clearly see the text or other visual element. Pick a spot that is about as far away as the furthest person will be during the presentation. Adjust the font's size or magnification as necessary in order to ensure that it will be clear to this person. If they can read it, everyone else who is closer should be able to as well.

Remember to use the Rule of Six when working with text on a slide. This means:

- No more than six lines per slide
- No more than six words per line

Although this is not absolute, it is a good guideline to remember. It prevents you from overloading your slide with too much information. Use the Notes Pane for detailed notes and keep your main slide as a high-level overview.

6.5: Coping with Stage Fright

Stage fright is the sometimes debilitating nervous feeling, that overcomes an individual when they are about to "take the stage" to deliver a presentation. Some presenters are better at handling it than others. The following list includes tips on how to cope with feelings of stage fright.

- **Preparation is Key:** Preparation for a business presentation includes lots of practise. This exhibits professionalism to the audience and minimizes stage fright.

- **No Acting:** Be yourself and use appropriate decorum.

- **Pep Talk:** Positive self-talk at the beginning will help you be successful in the presentation.

- **Invisible Mistakes:** Most audience members do not notice many of the small mistakes presenters commonly make. You are often the only person who knows that you have made a mistake. Do not point it out and tell them you have made a mistake. Move on.

- **Pre-Presentation Self-Care:** Get a good night's sleep before a business presentation, and eat before the presentation.

- **Slow Down and Set the Pace:** When nervous, most people speak at a faster rate than normal. Slow your rate of speech down. This demonstrates calm and professionalism to your audience. When you speak articulately and at a good pace, your audience will feel that you are the best person to give that presentation.

- **Watch your Audience:** If you are nervous, find a familiar face in the audience. Find the most comforting person and focus on him or her periodically.

- **Do Not Tell Audience:** Do not tell your audience you are nervous. Your audience will often lose confidence in you and start constructing a slightly less professional image of you. This sends the message that you are unprepared for your presentation.

- **Highlight Note Cards:** Small index cards with a couple notes on them are often useful during presentations. Occasionally glancing at your notes is acceptable. Highlight the important bullet points to make them easier to find.

- **Scripting:** You can consider writing out a script for the content that you want to deliver. A script does not have to have the exact wording of what you wish to say in your presentation, as long as the ideas you wish to communicate to your audience are clear.

With time and practise, most people will be able to manage their stage fright.

Chapter 6 Recap

As this chapter ends, it is time to review the key concepts detailed in Chapter 6 of this textbook:

- Preparation is the key to a successful business meeting, including timing, place, action items, and a detailed agenda.

- A prepared meeting leader is the starting point of any productive business meeting.

- It is critical to avoid problematic team dynamics such as monopolization, scapegoating, and groupthink. The first step to improving and avoiding such dynamics is understanding them.

- If a team lacks a strong leader, it is much more likely to experience problematic team dynamics and lack a clear and defined direction for projects.

- Positive team dynamics are the result of effective leader behaviours, the discussion of member roles and responsibilities early on in a project, employment of team-building activities, a clear meeting purpose, detailed planning, time management, and the adherence to informal rules of order.

- Misunderstanding in a business environment costs valuable time and money, which means the company is not operating at peak efficiency.

- Delivering an effective and professional presentation requires a lot of time and hard work.

- Give improved oral presentations by knowing your audience, practising as much as possible, contingency planning if technology should fail, and developing an appropriate presentation style.

- Visuals should clarify or enhance your words and not be the basis of your presentation.

- Time, practise, and experience help individuals cope with stage fright.

Chapter 6 Quiz

1. What is the key to a successful business meeting?

    a. Talking
    b. Preparation
    c. Going over time
    d. Ending early

2. _____ occurs when one person receives blame for the faults and wrongdoings of others.

    a. Scapegoating
    b. Non-participation
    c. Withdrawal
    d. None of the above

3. Which of the following should you not do to combat stage fright?

    a. Use highlighted note cards
    b. Accept your nervous feelings
    c. Tell the audience
    d. Move past mistakes

4. If deadlines are an issue, you should:

    a. Do nothing
    b. Extend the deadline
    c. Consider flex lines
    d. Always submit on the deadline no matter what

5. One person taking exclusive control over a team is engaging in what type of poor team dynamic:

    a. Non-Participation
    b. Conflict
    c. Monopolization
    d. Groupthink

6. Visuals should be the base of your presentation:

    a. True
    b. False

7. What is the Rule of Six?

    a. Six words per line
    b. Six lines per slide
    c. Six words per slide
    d. A and B

8. Groupthink occurs when all individuals express their opinions and the groups discuss them before finding the best solution.

    a. True
    b. False

Answers:

1. (B) 2. (A) 3. (C) 4. (C) 5. (C) 6. (B) 7. (D) 8. (B)

....
....
....
....
....
....
....
....
....
....
....
....
....
....
....
....
....

Making the Most of the Phone

The previous chapters on oral communication covered the development of basic professional oral communication skills and specific applications of oral communications in a business environment. This final chapter will focus on one of the most prevalent technologies in the professional world: the telephone.

Technology plays a significant role in business communication from written methods such as emails and memos, to oral methods like business presentations. The telephone is the most prevalent of these technologies not only because of the masses who use it on a daily basis, but also because of the variety of business uses.

Unfortunately, however, the telephone is often under-utilized and actually used incorrectly in business environments. Throughout this chapter, we will go over multiple aspects of conducting professional business over the telephone.

Learning Goals

- Implement professional practises before as well as during a business phone call.
- Understand how a conference call works and what to do in order to execute it smoothly.
- Create a professional voicemail greeting.
- Leave a good voicemail message on an answering machine.

my notes

7.1: Using a Telephone

The telephone allows users to connect with co-workers and customers easily and quickly. Conference calls allow you to connect with multiple clients and/ or coworkers simultaneously.

Before You Call

- **Time:** When preparing to call someone, ensure that you have sufficient time to discuss all the topics of your call. If your time is short, say so. If you require more time to fully discuss all topics, schedule another time, when you can speak at length.
    - In order to avoid feeling rushed, try scheduling in 5 or 10 minutes beyond what you think is necessary.
    - If you will call across different time zones, be sure to plan each call accordingly.

- **Necessary Information:** Prior to the call, make a list of everything you need to address.
    - This includes the phone number you will be dialling, the name of your contact person and their position, as well as your own contact information.
    - Whether you are using a landline or a cell phone will depend on the nature of your job and the situation. If you are using a cell phone for business purposes, let the other person know. If there is interference or the call is dropped, the reconnection will be a smoother process.
    - If you must leave a voice mail, ensure it is complete (your name, the reason for the call, a contact number, and a request for a call back, if necessary.)

- **Opening Statement:** When making a business phone call, there are two different types of opening statements that you need to prepare.
    - The first is when someone else other than your contact person picks up the phone. If this happens, you need to provide your contact's name, their position, and your information.
    - The second type of opening statement is when your contact person is the one to answer the phone. Start with a professional greeting such as "Hello," "Good morning/ afternoon," followed by "This is <insert your name>." At this point, allow the receiver to acknowledge you.

- **Pen and Paper:** Particularly with longer business calls, taking notes about the discussion is essential. We may confuse, or even forget, crucial information after the call. Avoid taking notes on a computer as the sound of a keyboard can be distracting.
    - Some of the items that could be of note during a conversation include a follow-up time to call, an in-person business meeting, documents that need to be exchanged, et cetera.

- **Questions:** Review any information regarding the topic prior to the phone call. Write down questions that you have that can be clarified during the phone conversation.
    - If there is no substantial information, consider at least listing some general questions about the topic. Be as specific as possible.

- **Voicemail:** When you make a call, you may reach your contact's voicemail. In the event that this happens, you need to be prepared to leave a message. Always remain professional when leaving a voicemail message. Details are provided later in this chapter.

Exercise

You are making a business phone call, and you reach the secretary of the person you are trying to contact. What is your greeting?

....

....

....

....

....

....

....

....

....

....

....

During the Call

During the call itself, you are still projecting an image of yourself and your company. You should come across as positive, professional, and organized. In order to achieve this, here are some helpful tips to keep in mind.

Quiet Environment

Ensure that you are in a quiet environment such as your office with the door closed, an empty conference room, or your own home if the call is after business hours. Never schedule a call for when you will be in the car, on public transit, or in another busy area like a mall or downtown. Your contact may find it difficult to hear you properly, making the call prone to misinterpretation. It also demonstrates a decreased level of professionalism.

If someone calls you unexpectedly and you are in a busy or noisy area, quickly explain your situation. Arrange to call back in a few minutes when you have found a quiet spot, or arrange to speak to them on another day when you can ensure a more controlled environment.

Not only will it be difficult to focus on the call in a distracting environment, you will be discussing company specific information. When you are in a public place, you do not know who is listening to your end of the call. You could be disclosing confidential or proprietary information without realizing it.

Positive Wording

It is always necessary to speak positively. This means to be direct, honest, and constructive in everything you say. Even if the topic covers a negative situation, such as company downsizing, you want to keep your message positive.

- Try to consider possible objections and concerns. Prepare solutions in advance.
- Do not try to make a bad situation sound better than it is. This is misleading, and may confuse your audience. Be honest and offer constructive comments. This will help you stay as positive as possible without misleading anyone.
- Focus on the issue, not on the individual. Do not make this about blaming someone. Identify what happened, why, what people learned from it, and how others can avoid it in the future.

No Personal Judgments

Phrases such as "I feel" and "I believe" are opinion-based, and often you cannot substantiate them. "I believe you wasted a lot of time today, and that's why the package went out late" is personal and blaming. Hold off on jumping to conclusions or any personal judgments of a situation. Try to see it from the other point of view as well.

Keep the comments and feedback quantifiable. Use specific and demonstrable examples, such as, "We received the shipment at 3:30pm on Thursday last week. However, according to our order, we were supposed to receive the shipment by 5:00pm on Wednesday. What happened to prevent the package from shipping on time?"

Reiterate Information

At the end of the phone call, briefly summarize any relevant information discussed during the call. Decisions made earlier in a call may be forgotten, so remember to review everything at the end.

This may include items such as documents to send, potential solutions, next steps, additional phone calls, and in-person meetings. Reviewing this information allows all parties to understand what they will need to do, as well as be aware of who is covering each element of the plan.

Gratitude

At the end of the conversation, thank your contact. Their time and energy is as valuable as yours is and making it known that you appreciate their time goes a long way.

Inbound Business Calls

You will often have scheduled business calls and will therefore expect your phone to ring. However, calls will sometimes come unexpectedly. The following strategies will help you keep on top of your work, while still handling calls.

- **Three Ring Rule:** Pick up the phone within three rings as often as you can. Many systems will automatically default to voicemail. This may frustrate the caller.

- **Greeting:** When you pick up the phone, greet the caller (e.g. hello, good morning, good afternoon), state your name, and ask the caller how you can help them.
    - This identifies you to the caller. They will know immediately whether or not you are the person to whom they need to speak.

- **After Greeting:** Once you have introduced yourself allow the caller to state who they are and the purpose of their call.

- **Focus on Solutions:** Find out what they need, if you can deliver it to them, or if you need to refer the problem to someone else. Keep the client's perspective in mind. The interaction may be the only time the customer interacts with the company. They will form an impression of you and the overall company.

7.2: Conference Calling

There are times in which two or more parties need to have a meeting and are unable to meet in person due to time or travel constraints. A conference call allows all parties to meet and discuss their issues. You can also combine conference calls with webinars.

How to Execute a Professional Conference Call

Successful conference calls are organized and well planned. You need to know who must attend and what everyone needs to discuss.

Scheduling the Conference Call
The first step is to schedule the conference call at the most convenient time for your participants. A good practice is to organize the meeting to fit the schedule of the most important person on the call, or the person who could be the most difficult to schedule. Send a meeting request to all required attendees, stating the time, date, and subject of the call.

On The Agenda

Next, create a detailed agenda to follow during the call. The following list is a selection of questions to ask when creating an agenda for a conference call. Note that this list is not all-inclusive, but it will get you started.

- What is the main purpose behind this call?

- How much time will each section take?
  - Example: 5 minutes for all introductions

- Who will lead each section?

- What sections will the call require?
  - Introductions
  - Question and Answer
  - Summary/Review

Punctuality

A conference call, just as any other business meeting, must begin and end on time. The meeting leader should start the call on time and all participants should dial in on time. If a participant calls in late, do not back track to repeat information. The individual can catch up after the call or can review the minutes when they are distributed. If this is the first call of a series, ensure that all participants are aware of the expectations.

Location

When you participate in a conference call, either as a leader or as a participant, ensure that you are in a quiet environment with no distractions. A phone amplifies external noise, and others around you do not need to hear the call. If multiple participants from the same office are involved in the call, try to call from one phone, rather than dialing in from multiple phones.

Ensure that all required technology, such as a laptop or tablet computer, is available during the conference call. If your call is part of a webinar, you may need to log in to a service or watch a presentation on screen.

Notes

Keep a pen and paper handy to take notes during the meeting. Taking notes during a conference call helps to retain information not only about the main issue discussed during the call, but also the finer details. Additionally, taking notes throughout the conference call is good preparation for the scheduled summary period at the end of the call.

Record

If you need to make verbatim notes following the conference call, use an audio recording device during the call. Make sure that all participants are aware that this is in place, and are aware of how people can use the recording after the call has concluded.

Keep To Time

Successful conference calls keep to the allotted time for the meeting. In the agenda, you scheduled in the total time that the meeting would take, as well as budgeted time slots for each section of the conference call.

Remember that everyone participating in this call is taking time out of his or her day to participate. In certain cases, such as in sales positions, brokerage houses, and accounting firms, time is literally money. When someone is not doing their job, they are not making money. Be respectful of participant's time. If you are not, these individuals will be less likely to participate in the future.

No Multitasking

During the conference call, eliminate all distractions so your sole focus is the call. This includes, but is not limited to, sending emails or text messages, logging on to Facebook or other social media websites, or working on any other work at your desk. This distracts you as a listener, and is disrespectful to the other conference call participants. The only activities you should undertake during a conference call are taking notes or looking at any supplementary material the speakers may have provided.

Limit Participants

Conference calls can sometimes get chaotic and confusing. Often times many people will try to speak at once, and it can be difficult to identify who is speaking. As well, people with stronger personalities can try to talk over one another. Establish the "one person speaking at a time" rule. The call leader will ensure that no one tries to talk over others. Also, have people identify themselves when their turn arrives.

Keep On Topic

The call should focus on the agenda. If the discussion starts to deviate, the meeting leader should refer back to the agenda. If a topic arises that the leader did not include in the agenda, move it to the open forum period (if there is one), or include it in a future meeting. This will reduce confusion during note taking, and eliminate any extraneous discussions.

Summarize

At the end of every conference call, summarize the main issues discussed, including any solutions or next steps. This allows all of the participants to review their notes and ensure that they have all the necessary information. If they do not have the required information, this period allows them to fill in gaps.

7.3: Voicemails

Voicemail is another effective professional tool. There will be times you, or the person you are calling, will not be able to answer the phone. When this happens, it is essential to know how to conduct yourself using voicemail.

Voicemail is a secure tool as messages are only accessible to the recipient, since they arrive in one voicemail account. In addition, some voicemail machines will keep the messages up to seven days, so the recipient can listen to it as often as necessary during that time.

Professional Voicemail Greeting

Ensure you have a complete, professional greeting. This greeting includes your full name, your extension, your title/position, status (in the office, away, in meetings all day, et cetera), and details required from the caller (full name, message, and callback number).

Tell the caller when they can expect a call back. The generally accepted time frame for a call back is within 24 hours. Provide a contact name for immediate assistance if you will be away from your desk for an extended period and will not be able to check voicemails or return calls. Instances in which you will need to use a contact name include vacation time, out of office training, and when you are away on business.

Some organizations require you to update your voicemail every day, and include the current date. Confirm what your supervisor expects of you.

Exercise

You are the marketing assistant in a company called Green Tea Marketing. Create two voicemail greetings: one for when you are in the office, but away from your phone, and one for when you are away for two weeks on vacation.

....
....
....
....
....
....
....
....
....
....

Leaving a Message

Whenever you make a phone call, be prepared ahead of time for two different conversations: one you would have when speaking to a live person and a condensed message you would leave in their voicemail. If you reach their voicemail, here are some tips:

1. Have a professional greeting prepared if your call goes to voicemail.

2. Include your full name and call back phone number if you require a call back.

3. State the purpose of your call.

4. Keep the message short. Information could be lost in the shuffle if you try to include too much in one message.

5. Include your whole message and identify if you would like a call back.

Overall, when you reach a person's voicemail, it is essential to remain professional, polite, and organized.

Chapter 7 Recap

Before moving on to the last quiz, let us recap the key ideas from this chapter:

- Before you place a business call, set aside the time and come prepared with the necessary information and an opening statement.

- Taking notes with a pen and paper during a phone call is encouraged, particularly during long and detailed conversations.

- Reserve time at the end of the call to ask some questions about the topics covered and any potential next steps.

- Remain positive, professional, and organized during all business phone calls.

- Place your business calls from a quiet environment.

- Use positive wording during the phone call, but do not misrepresent negative situations.

- Keep your comments and feedback quantifiable and free of personal judgements.

- At the end of the phone call, briefly summarize any relevant information discussed.

- At the end of the conversation, express your gratitude towards your contact.

- Pick up the phone within three rings. After you greet the caller, let them state their name and purpose for calling.

- Focus on solutions when responding to a caller, even if you have to transfer the call to someone better equipped to help.

- Professional conference calls require scheduling, a detailed agenda, punctual attendees, and a quiet location for each participant.

- When participating in or leading a conference call, consider taking notes or recording the conversation.

- Do not multitask during a conference call as it is distracting to you and the other participants.

- A professional voicemail greeting includes your full name, your extension, your title/position, status (in the office, away, in meetings all day, et cetera), and details required from the caller (full name, message, and callback number).

- Prepare for a phone call ahead of time, with two different potential conversations: one you would have when speaking to a live person and a condensed message you would leave in their voicemail.

Chapter 7 Quiz

1. Location does not matter during a conference call. You can participate from anywhere.

    a. True
    b. False

2. How many types of opening statements do you need to prepare before you call?

    a. 3
    b. 2
    c. 1
    d. 4

3. You should always schedule business phone calls.

    a. True
    b. False

4. When a participant arrives late to a conference call, it:

    a. Is professional
    b. Doesn't make a difference either way
    c. Disrupts the call
    d. Is expected

5. When receiving a business call, you should never:

    a. Say you cannot help the client
    b. Transfer their call to another department
    c. Wait three rings to pick up
    d. A and C

6. You should be prepared with a pen and paper to take notes during all situations described in this chapter.

    a. False
    b. True

Answers:

1. (B, need quiet environment) 2. (B) 3. (A) 4. (C) 5. (A) 6. (B)

A

Abstract noun: Qualities or ideas that do not "exist" physically (e.g. kindness, beauty).

Active listening: An oral communication technique where the listener makes an effort to fully understand the speaker's verbal and nonverbal signals by providing feedback and paraphrasing speech.

Active voice: A grammatical voice in which the subject of the sentence performs the action expressed in the verb.

Adjective phrase: A group of words in which the adjective is the main word.

Adjective: A word that modifies and describes a noun. You have a *lovely* home.

Adverb: A word that modifies and intensifies a verb, noun, adjective, or another adverb. Adverbs often end in –ly, and usually answer the question "how" in some way. She ran *quickly*.

Agenda: A detailed schedule of items to discuss during a formal meeting or a conference call.

Analytical report: A report written to identify a particular problem and recommend a solution.

Antecedent: A word, phrase, or clause replaced by a pronoun or other substitute later in the same or subsequent sentence(s).

Apostrophe: (') A punctuation mark used to make contractions, or put words in a possessive case.

Appendix: A portion of a report/proposal that includes auxiliary information the reader may find interesting, but interrupts the flow of the rest of the piece (charts, technical terminology, et cetera.) Placed at the end of the document.

Argumentative writing: A writing style used to make and support an argument, either for or against something. Its most common use is in legal writing, academics, and critical essays.

B

Body language: A method of non-verbal communication through body movements done both consciously as well as unconsciously.

Business plan: A formal statement of business goals. It must outline why the goals are attainable, what kind of steps will be taken, et cetera.

C

Chunking: A process of speed reading that involves combining lines, sentences, and phrases, usually by mentally removing articles like "the," "a," "an," and "to be."

Colloquialism: A phrase, word, or saying that is often specific to a culture or language.

Colon: (:) Punctuation used for listing nouns and adjectives. Everything after the colon must compliment what comes before the colon.

Comma: (,) A punctuation mark used to separate clauses, words, and phrases into a particular order.

Common noun: The name of a general thing, as opposed to a proper noun—a name given to something. *Car, tree, desk.*

Complex sentence: A sentence containing an independent clause and at least one dependent clause.

Compound noun: A noun composed of two or more nouns. "A gas station." "A football."

Compound sentence: A sentence with multiple independent clauses and no dependent clauses.

Compound-complex sentence: A sentence with multiple independent clauses and at least one dependent clause.

Conference call: In business, this is when more than two people are having a meeting through the telephone.

Conflict resolution: A problem-solving process of accountability, firmness, shared goals, and open communication.

Conflict: An argument between two or more individuals.

Conjunction: A conjunction is a word used to connect independent clauses *and, but,* and *if,* among others.

Constructive feedback: Providing directions for improvement in balance with positive reinforcement so the individual has information with which they are able to work.

Critical reading: Refuting or agreeing with claims after evaluating the argument of a text you are reading; not taking everything as true and making your own decisions after further thinking and research.

Cultural differences: This can result when communicating with people of other cultures.

D

Definite article: One of two articles in the English language, the word *the* is used to name something specific.

Dependent clause: A clause that cannot make its own grammatically correct sentence and must have an independent clause supporting it.

Digital literacy: A set of skills for using the Internet effectively for working, communicating, and researching.

Discrimination: Unfair treatment of a person/people based on their gender, age, sexual orientation, race, creed, or social status.

Discussion of findings: The longest part of a formal report. This is where you will explain the facts leading up to your conclusion and/or recommendations.

E

Ethics: A set of guidelines for moral conduct. Applied ethics are ethics that are upheld by professionals and usually enforced by a code of conduct (medical ethics, business ethics, and environmental ethics).

Ethnocentrism: The belief that one group of people (race/ethnicity) is superior to another.

Executive summary: The key points of a formal report, established after a report's introduction.

Extensive reading: Reading for pleasure; builds on skills learned by intensive reading while deepening one's understanding of language.

F

Filtering: Deciding what is most important and only trying to retain that information—letting everything else fall to the wayside.

Font: The appearance of written type.

G

Gerund: A verb that can be used as a noun when the suffix "-ing" is attached to the end. *I miss my grandmother's cooking.*

Global editing: Revising a piece of writing as a whole. In this stage, you look at paragraph structure, purpose, and level of diction.

Groupthink: The method of thinking and making decisions as a group that discourages individual creativity, responsibility, and expression of ideas.

I

Impression management: Ways in which people and organizations influence others' perception of them.

Indefinite article: A word that indicates a non-specific thing: the words *a* and *an*.

Independent clause: A clause that can stand alone as its own sentence and still make grammatical sense.

Informal report: A routine, usually brief report that is used for data compilation and internal matters.

Informational report: Objectively relays data and information about a specific problem or process. These are often internally written and circulated.

Intensive reading: The exhaustive process in which attention is given to grammar, syntax, and other technical aspects of language.

Intercultural communication: The form of communicating across cultural and social groups.

Inter-office: Pertaining to interactions between offices (proposal, billing for services, et cetera).

Interrogative pronoun: A pronoun that posits a question *who, what, where, when, why, how.*

Intransitive verbs: Do not take an object, but express actions that do not require the subject to do another action.

Intra-office: Pertaining to interactions within one office (memos, scheduling, project management, et cetera).

Italics: A typeface used for emphasis, titles, and untranslated foreign words.

L

Letter of transmittal: The portion of a proposal that adds a personal touch. It is your greeting to the person reading the proposal.

LinkedIn: A social network geared towards professionals. You can find employers and fellow colleagues in your field, and many other networking opportunities.

Linking verbs: Verbs that explain the link between the subject and rest of the sentence (usually a form of "to be").

Local editing: Editing for grammar, tense continuity, and other factors.

M

Monopolization: one person taking exclusive control over the meeting and agenda, often forcing their own agenda on the team.

Multitasking listening: Planning your response while the speaker is still talking.

Muscle reading: A nine step process to practice reading comprehension and retention.

N

Non-participation/Withdrawal: One or more people stop or are not participating in problem solving or team discussions.

Nonverbal communication: The process of sending messages between people through wordless cues such as body language, posture, eye movements, and paralinguistics.

P

Paralinguistics: The non-lexical elements of language and speech, including tone, pitch and volume, fluency, and rate of speaking.

Participles: Verbs that function as an adjective by adding either an "-ed" or "-ing" suffix to the end of the verb.

Period: (.) A punctuation mark used to indicate the end of a sentence.

Glossary of Terms

Persuasive writing: Writing intended to sway an audience to a particular idea, purchase a product, or anything else requiring persuasion.

Plagiarism: The misappropriation, either intentional or not, of material that you did not write yourself. There are many legal, professional, and ethical problems with miscrediting others' work.

Postpositive adjective: An adjective that appears after a noun, and usually used for poetic and artistic purposes.

Predicate: The action or description of the subject in a sentence.

Prefix: Sets of letters used at the beginning of a word to change its meaning.

Preposition: Words that indicate location, position, and time.

Pronoun: A word that substitutes a noun. There are many different kinds of pronouns, including subject, reciprocal, indefinite, and object pronouns.

Proofreading: The stage of editing where you will pay close attention to grammar, punctuation, and other small mistakes.

Proper noun: A noun, capitalized, used to address a specific person, place, or thing.

Proposal: A piece of work written to offer or request a service, partnership, or other products and services between companies (or within one).

Protocol: A list of rules that act as the official method of conducting business.

R

Reading comprehension: The ability to read text and process its meaning.

Reference: A way to direct your reader to where you got your information. There are many reference style guides, so make sure you know which is standard for your company.

S

Salutation: The first lines you will write in an email to greet the recipient. You should write these with attention to who you wish to address and the email's purpose.

Scanning: A reading technique that involves going through a block of text (or icons, or symbols), to find information relevant to your immediate purpose.

Scapegoating: When an individual is blamed for the faults or wrongdoings of others. This is a common source of conflict within teams.

Selective listening: A technique for listening that filters information in order to achieve comprehension.

Semicolon: (;) A punctuation mark used to link closely related clauses.

Simple sentence: A sentence with one independent clause and no dependent clause(s).

Skimming: Involves reading through a text quickly to understand the general idea instead of more specific points.

Slang: Informal language used by a specific group of people. profession, et cetera. Usually refers to specific words, but can include longer phrases. It is more common in speech than in writing.

Slug: A very brief summary format for articles, folders, et cetera. The format varies often, but the one used in this book is removing spaces and capitalizing the first letter of each word (e.g. "BusinessCommunicationsBook").

Social media: Content that is shared by social networks. This can include videos, text, images, and many other media.

Social networking: Interacting and connecting via websites that share social media (Facebook, Twitter, Pinterest, etc.).

Speed reading: A skill of reading rapidly and above the average speed of 200 to 400 words per minute.

Spreadsheet: A computer application for collecting, storing, analyzing, and processing data.

Stage fright: The feeling of nervousness prior to a business presentation, performance, or other public speaking scenario.

Subject: The person or object that acts in a sentence.

Subject line: The line in an email that indicates what the email is regarding.

Subject-verb agreement: A grammar rule that ensures that the arrangement of the subject, verb, and object is grammatically correct.

Subvocalization: The voice in the back of your head that you hear repeating the words you read. This is also when you subconsciously move your mouth to the words you read.

Suffix: A set of letters added at the end of a word that modifies the word.

T

Team dynamics: The behavioral forces that exert influence over the team's performance and effectiveness.

Tense: The period of time in which a verb takes place (past, present, future).

Three Ring Rule: The professional practice of picking up the phone after no more than three rings in a business scenario.

Transitive verb: These verbs take the action of the subject and apply it to the object.

Keyword Index

Keyword Index

A | Appendix

Grammar and Punctuation in a Nutshell

Parts of Speech

Nouns

A noun is a person, place, or thing.

dog, cat, house, sky, girl

Proper Nouns
Proper nouns use a capital and identify someone or something specific.

Name: Emily, Susan, Bill
Place: Toronto, London
Date: Wednesday, Christmas, January
Thing: GM, Canada Post

Pronouns
These are words that take the place of a noun.

Personal pronouns:	I, you, she, he, they
Reflexive pronouns:	Himself, herself, yourself, yourselves, myself, itself, ourselves
Intensive pronouns:	Myself, yourself, yourselves, himself, herself, itself, ourselves
Relative pronouns:	That, which, who, whom, whose
Interrogative pronouns:	Who? Whom? What? Which? Whoever?
Indefinite pronouns:	Somebody, something, nobody, no one, anyone, anybody

Count vs. Non-Count Nouns

Count nouns are those things that can be counted. Non-count nouns usually are things that cannot be counted.

> Count: Telephone
> Non-Count: Information

Count vs. Non-Count Nouns Exercise

Put a checkmark in either box, for either count or non-count.

Term	Count	Non-Count
Assignment		
Vocabulary		
Candidate		
Honesty		
Letter		
Homework		

Adjectives

These are words that describe, qualify, or modify a noun or pronoun. An adjective precedes the noun or pronoun in a sentence. There can be more than two adjectives qualifying a single noun.

Limiting Adjectives

This adjective is limited to the noun or pronoun it describes.

- Possessive adjectives: his, her, my, its, our, you, theirs
- Demonstrative: this, that, these, those
- Numerical: three, ten, five, tenfold
- Indefinite: any, all, some, a few
- Interrogative: which, where, who

Descriptive Adjectives

- A word or words that use an attribute or attributes to describe the noun or pronoun.

- A simple adjective is one word used to describe the noun or pronoun: pretty, quaint, et cetera.
- A compound adjective is a two-word combination used to describe the noun or pronoun: short-sighted, middle-aged, et cetera.

Verbs

This is the action word in the sentence. It states the action being performed or the state of being. A verb can be one or more words, depending on its tense.

Raging
Was raging
Had been raging

Transitive Verbs
These verbs have an object as a recipient.

The dog *ate* the food.

Intransitive Verbs
There is no object receiving the action.

The wind *howled* ferociously.

Linking Verbs
Express a state of being, not a state of action.

Elizabeth II *became* Queen upon her father's death.

Adverbs

An adverb describes or modifies the verb, the adjective or another adverb.

Finally demonstrated
Rather good
Very logically and precisely

These describe:

Place answers the question: where? here? there? in? out? down? up?
Time answers the question: when? now? later? earlier?
Manner answers the question: how carefully? precisely? slowly? fast?
Degree answers the question: to what extent? very? surely? completely?
Inference and result asks how to join an idea: therefore? thus? consequently?

Interrogative asks questions that cannot be answered yes or no: where? what? when? where?

Adjectives and Adverbs Exercise

Identify each adjective or an adverb. Determine if it is being used correctly. If it is not correct, correct it.

1. "Drive carefully – these roads can be dangerous."
2. "The dog ran so fast that the owner could not keep up with it."
3. "Everything is going swimmingly."
4. "Mrs. Parker bakes the best cookies."
5. "He was too short to reach the top shelf."
6. "It was extremely hot yesterday."

Articles

These are words that also describe the noun or pronoun. For example: "a, an, the." There are *indefinite* and *definite* articles: an indefinite article is either "a" or "an," and the only definite article in English is "the."

A or An Exercise

In the following phrases, supply either "a" or "an":

1. ___ problem
2. ___ elephant
3. ___ trainyard
4. ___ apple
5. ___ coconut
6. ___ exercise

Prepositions

This type of word shows the relationship between a noun or pronoun and other words in a sentence.

Prepositions can include words such as:

about	above	according to	across
after	against	along	along with
among	apart from	around	as
as for	at	because of	before
behind	below	beneath	beside
between	beyond	but	by
by means of	concerning	despite	down
during	except	except for	excepting
for	from	in	in addition to
in back of	in case of	in front of	in place of
inside	in spite of	instead of	into
like	near	next	of
off	on	onto	on top of
out	out of	outside	over
past	regarding	round	since
through	throughout	till	to
toward	under	underneath	unlike
until	up	upon	up to
with	within	without	

Subject-Verb Agreement Exercise

Underline the subjects once and the verbs twice. If the subjects and verbs do not agree, change the verbs to match the subjects.

1. The children was paying attention to the teacher.
2. James and Mike are driving to Toronto for the Blue Jays game.
3. The stores were all closed on Labour Day.
4. Nick and Bilay has to work on Saturday.
5. My friend and I are going swimming.
6. Janelle and Bill walks to the grocery store.
7. They forgive her after the argument yesterday.
8. Erin and her mother have too many pets.

Conjunctions

These words connect sentences or parts of sentences together. They are:

And, But, Or, Nor, For, So, Yet

Coordinating conjunctions join sentences and independent clauses (full sentences that can stand by themselves).

Subordinating conjunctions join a full independent clause (a sentence that can stand by itself) and a dependent clause (a partial sentence that cannot stand independently).

After, Although, As, Because, How, If, Once, Since, That, Though, Till, Until, When, Where, While

Interjections

Interjections are specifically designed to express emotions, such as pain, surprise, or anger. They do not relate grammatically to other parts of the sentence.

Ouch! Oh! Alas!
That test was hard, huh?
Oh no, did that hurt?

Sentence Construction (Syntax)

Sentence construction, or syntax, determines whether a sentence is a simple sentence, a complex sentence, or a compound sentence.

Simple Sentences

A *simple sentence* is one complete thought containing a subject and a predicate.

The *subject* of the sentence is a noun and usually appears at the beginning of the sentence. The *predicate* within the sentence describes what the subject does or what it is like.

A *complex predicate* consists of the complete verb and any modifiers.

> The boy *caught* and *dropped* the ball.

A *simple predicate* consists of a complete verb.

> I *slept* in my bed.

The *direct object* is the word (or group of words) that receive the action. It answers the questions "who" or "what" after the verb.

> The winner *accepted* the award.

The *indirect object* comes before the object, and describes to whom or from whom the action is received.

> She lent *us* money.

The *complement* follows a linking verb to complete its meaning and may be a predicate noun or adjective.

> He is a *bully*.

A *predicate adjective* modifies the subject of the verb.

> The panic was *widespread*.

A modifier is a word or group of words that limits a noun, a verb, or a thought. It may be an adjective, adverb, prepositional phrase, participle, participle phrase, or infinitive phrase.

> The girl with the *high* cheek bones wore her hair up today.
> The *contaminated* areas are *quarantined*.
> The fire raged *wildly*.
> The pitcher with the *sprained shoulder* grimaced with pain.
> Your *limp* hair is not very *attractive*.
> In order to *win*, you have to *play*.

Compound Sentences

A compound sentence is created when two independent (main) clauses are joined with a coordinating conjunction.

but, or, however, and, neither, either, nor, yet, also

Complex Sentences

A *complex sentence* has one independent clause and one or more subordinate clauses (which can be adjectival, noun, or adverbial).

A *subordinate clause* is not a sentence on its own, and cannot stand independently.

An *adjectival clause* modifies the noun or pronoun, like an adjective. This statement is introduced by a relative pronoun: who, which, or that.

An *adverbial clause* modifies the verb, like an adverb. It modifies a verb, noun or adjective and answers the questions when, why, to what extent, on what condition and how.

A *subordinating conjunction* introduces adverbial clauses expressing a relationship of time after, before, until, when, whenever, while, as, place here, there, cause as, because, since, when, manner, degree, result that, so that, in order that, condition if, thus, provided that, or concession though, although, even though, notwithstanding that.

A *noun clause* behaves the same way as a noun. Noun clauses are introduced by words such as: that, who, what, why, when, whether.

Compound-Complex Sentences

This sentence has two or more independent clauses and one or more subordinate clauses.

Simple, Complex, and Compound Sentences Exercise

Identify each type of sentence. Write Simple, Complex, or Compound beside the sentence.

1. Alan took the dog to the dog park.
2. I wanted to go to the movies, but I had to save money.
3. Lisa called in sick today.
4. Just remember, what goes around comes around.
5. There are three levels of the Canadian government: legislative, executive, and judicial.

6. The boy's mother looked frustrated.

7. The car wouldn't start, and Rick thought it might be the battery.

8. My friend's house is larger and nicer than mine.

Sentence Fragments

A sentence fragment is an incomplete sentence. The first word will start with a capital letter and the sentence ends with a period, question mark, or exclamation point. However, the thought is incomplete.

Sentence Fragments Exercise

Rewrite the following sentences so they are correct.

1. When I went to Paris. The weather was great for the whole trip.

2. There was a large barn. In the distance.

3. I was late. Because of the bus.

4. As soon as I get home. Wash the dishes.

5. I am going to Australia. Where the weather is warmer.

6. The Ontario government made an announcement. That they would be increasing the minimum wage.

7. Newspapers are falling out of fashion. In exchange for online news sources.

8. Mr. Jameson walked down the street. The wind in his hair.

Common Problem Words

Affect vs. Effect

Affect (v) means "to influence." Effect (n) means "result." There are times you may see effect used as a verb that means "to cause" and affect used as a noun that means "emotion." The rule-of-thumb is to use affect when you need to show action and effect when you describe someone/thing.

Between vs. Among

Use *between* when referring to two objects or people. Use *among* when you're talking about more than two objects or people.

Its vs. It's

Its is the possessive form of "it." It's is the contracted form of "it is" or "it has."

That vs. Which

Use *that* in order to single something out. Commas are not used with that. Use *which* if the clause is non-essential to the sentence. Commas are used only with which, as there is a pause.

Read your sentence out loud. Do you pause before or after the clause?

Subject-Verb Agreements

Your subject and verb should always agree—singular, plural, et cetera. When the clause that modifies the noun (the relative clause) begins with "one of", the verb within the clause should be plural. If two or more nouns are joined by "and" (compounds), use singular verbs.

Note: Each, either, everyone, everybody, neither, nobody, and someone are singular.

Punctuation

Commas

Use a comma to separate two complete ideas or clauses. Note: Read your sentence out loud. If you pause, insert a comma.

Parenthetical Clauses
You can also use commas around a parenthetical clause—one that could also be found in parentheses.

Compound Sentences
Place a comma before the conjunction in a compound sentence. Conjunctions—such as and, but, or because—are used to connect two independent clauses.

Remember: An independent clause is a sentence on its own, containing its own subject and verb. It is a complete thought by itself.

Comma Exercise

Correct *any* comma errors.

1. I had fun at the concert but the weather, was terrible.
2. Rachel and I, are going to the mall.
3. Green onions, peppers, and celery, are found in many Cajun foods.
4. She called me, to tell me the good news.
5. Thanks Jennifer for your hard work and dedication.
6. He was being a real jerk, last night.
7. I told you, to turn that music down!

Semicolons

Use a semicolon between two independent clauses not connected by a conjunction to indicate a close relationship between the ideas. You would otherwise use a period.

You should also use a semicolon if the two clauses are separated by an adverb. Do not use a semicolon to separate an independent and dependent clause.

Semicolon Use in Lists
Within lists, semicolons can be used in place of commas, even when individual items are more than one word.

Semicolon Exercise

Correct *any* semicolon errors in the following sentences.

1. I told you several times; that does not belong there.
2. It's only a matter of time; the city will pass a new law on skateboarding.
3. His bike tire went flat; he was upset.
4. Mammals come in many forms, for example, a whale is a mammal.
5. I have been to Montreal, Toronto, Halifax, London, Windsor and Guelph.

Colons

Use a colon to introduce a dependent clause (or a phrase or word) that answers an implied question, or introduce a list of related items. It is generally preceded by an independent clause.

> This is the latest in the current trend: creating our own documentation. You need to bring the following items: pen, pencil, eraser, whiteout, and paper.

Quotation Marks

Quotation marks are the inverted commas (" ") which surround a quote, a speech, or a literal title or name, and can be used to indicate a different—and ironic—meaning of a word or phrase than the one typically associated with it.

Periods and commas always go inside quotation marks. Punctuation such as question marks are also placed within the quotation marks if the question is enclosed in quotation marks.

> I asked, "Are you still my friend?"
> Do you agree with the statement "What's good for the goose is good for the gander?"

Single quotation marks are used for quotes within quotes and the period goes inside all quote marks.

> He replied, "Danea said, 'Do not treat me that way.'"

Use quotation marks to set off a direct quotation only.

> "When will you be here?" he asked.
> Note: This can also be written as: He asked, "When you will be there?"

Do not use quotation marks with a quote that is more than three lines long.

When you are quoting material containing spelling or grammar mistakes, use sic in italics and enclosed in square brackets to tell the reader that this is how the original material stated the information.

> The e-mail stated, "I will attend to [sic] if my schedule permits."

Apostrophes

An apostrophe can be used in a number of ways in the English language.

Contractions
Place the apostrophe where the letter has been removed.

> don't, isn't, you're, she's

Possession
Place the apostrophe before the s to show singular possession. If the word ends in an s, place the apostrophe after the s with no additional letters.

> one girl's dress, one child's book, Mr. James' jacket, Ms. Peters' calendar

Replacing Nouns
Place an apostrophe where the noun is implied.

> That is her sister's, not her, album.

Plural Possession
To create a plural possession, pluralise the noun and then use an apostrophe.

> two students' textbooks, the children's games

Plural Names
Do not use an apostrophe in the plural of a name.

> the Joneses in Scarborough
> the Smiths from Melbourne

Singular Compound Noun Possession
The apostrophe and the s show possession.

> in my sister-in-law's house

Plural Compound Noun Possession
Pluralize the compound noun first, then insert the apostrophe.

My two in-laws' vacation went well.

Multiple Possessions
If two people possess the same item, use the apostrophe and s after the second name only.

Stuart and Frank's company will be twice as successful next year.

However, if each item is separate, use the apostrophe and s after each name.

Claire's and John's classrooms need major renovations.

Apostrophes Exercise

Correct *any* apostrophe errors.

1. Kate left Andrews backpack on the bus.
2. Smartphone's have gotten much more affordable in the past few years.
3. Mr. Jones garden is beautiful.
4. The boys shirt was not tucked in like it should have been.
5. Its my life, Ill do what I want with it.
6. There are a great number of bear's in the provincial park.
7. Summers almost done and its time to go back to school.
8. The blister hurt Ramons foot.

Possessive Pronouns
Possessive pronouns such as his, hers, its, theirs, ours, yours, and whose, already show possession, therefore do not require an apostrophe.

That purse is mine, not yours.

Pronouns Exercise

Select from the following words to complete each of the sentences below: Me, myself, I, themselves, yourselves, ourselves, himself, herself, each other, itself.

1. He made a fool of _____ at the work party.
2. Take care of _____, because Chicago can be a dangerous city.
3. I did most of the work _____ while Rosa sat around and did nothing.
4. She takes _____ too seriously sometimes.

5. You look so regal tonight, like the Queen _____.
6. Help _____ to the beer in the fridge.
7. John knew how to defend _____.
8. By _____, that part is useless.

It Is/It Has

Only use "it's" when it is a contraction for it is or it has.

> It's so cold outside.
> It's been a great vacation.

Abbreviations

The plurals for abbreviations are used as nouns and do not require apostrophes.

> This company interviewed three PhDs before selecting the best candidate.

However, to show possession, put the apostrophe on the outside of the plural.

> The four PhDs' combined knowledge is invaluable to the company.

You do not need an apostrophe for a plural of non-abbreviation combinations.

> Learning your ABCs is done when you're young.

Italics

Italics are slanted typefaces that have many uses. They can be used when writing out the title of a movie, book, publication, journal, or other media (except for television episodes, short stories, and articles), binomial nomenclature in the natural sciences, and for emphasis.

> *Of Mice and Men* is a classic book. (title)
> I can't *believe* he'd do something like that! (emphasis)
> The binomial name of the common raccoon is *Procyon lotor*.

Exclamation Points

The exclamation point (!) shows emphasis or surprise. It is not typically used in formal business writing.

Ellipsis Marks

Ellipsis (...) are used when you omit information (such as a word, phrase, et cetera) from a quote. Typically, three dots represent removed material.

Three Dot Method
Use three dots (periods) when you've removed information in the middle of a sentence or between sentences. Leave out punctuation such as commas that were in the original text. Also, the three periods should always go within square brackets.

> "[…] We choose this time, because it is a time, of all others, when Want is keenly felt, and Abundance rejoices." Charles Dickens, A Christmas Carol.

> "Constitutional monarchy […] is a form of government in which a monarch acts as head of state within the parameters of a constitution [...]"

Also, use the three dots that end the preceding paragraph(s) when you omit one or more paragraphs within a long quotation.

Periods

A period (.) goes at the end of a complete sentence.

If the last word—such as an abbreviation like M.D. or etc.—in the sentence ends in a period, do not follow it with another period.

Insert a period after an indirect question.

> He asked where his key was.

Question Marks

A question mark (?) follows a direct question.

> Do you agree?

If the sentence is half statement and half question, it ends with a question mark.

> You like winning, don't you?

Spacing with Punctuation

A period, comma, semicolon, colon, exclamation point, question mark, and quotation mark require one space (press SPACEBAR once) after. Follow punctuation with two spaces when using a fixed-pitch font on typewriters and with some word processors.

There should be NO space on either side of a hyphen or em dash.

Dashes

En Dash

An en dash (-)is the width of the letter "n" and is used with dates. It is used in place of a hyphen or the word "to." Do not use spaces around the en dash.

> 1980-1989, Monday-Friday, university-alumni event.

Em Dash

An em dash (—) is the width of the letter "m." The em dash is usually used in informal writing as a stand-in for commas, semicolons, colons, and parentheses. It is used to add emphasis as an abrupt change in the logic of the sentence. You should use an em dash sparingly in formal writing.

> You are the person—the only employee company wide—who volunteered to take this project.

> You are the only one qualified to do this job—no one else could do it.

Punctuation Exercise

Place semicolons, dashes, colons, quotation marks, italics (use an underline), and parentheses where needed in the following sentences.

1. The film The Apartment is known for its morbid humour and excellent performances.
2. The following people are under investigation Joel McCraven Linda Hardt and Hank Stockton.
3. My teacher who is always late for class got upset with me for being late yesterday.
4. I enjoyed the Toronto Star article about the best neighbourhoods for young people.
5. Sure, said Bill, I can do that.
6. He went to the library to study even on weekends except on Sunday when he had swim team practice.
7. Shakespeare wrote To thine one self be true in his play Hamlet.

Parentheses

Parentheses (brackets) are another way of inserting secondary material to a thought—material non-essential, but useful, when explaining a thought. Parentheses contain material which, if removed, will not impact the audience's understanding of the main message. Including this information helps the audience, but is not critical.

> Travelling in the wintertime is harder than at other times of the year (in my opinion and personal experience), because you have to factor in the climate of the country to which you are travelling.

A parenthetical statement can almost sound like a footnote and does not have to be perfectly integrated into a sentence.

> The tsunami of grief ('tsunami' here meaning the overwhelming emotion felt by the woman) when her dog died seemed completely appropriate, considering how much her animal companions mean to her.

Parentheses can also enclose full sentences, in which case the period goes inside the closing parenthesis.

> I cannot have a dog in my apartment. (My landlords do not like them.)

If the parenthetical statement comes at the end of a sentence, but is not the whole sentence, the period or other punctuation mark goes outside the closing parenthesis.

> High heels are painful and pinch your feet (in my personal experience).

Plurals

Regular Plurals
A noun is made a regular plural when you add an 's.'

> boys and girls

The word is still a regular plural for words ending in sh, ch, s, z, or x. In this case, you add 'es' to the end to make it plural.

> churches

When a word ends in [consonant] + y, change 'y' to 'ie' and add 's.'

> *country* becomes *countries*

In compound nouns, the principal word becomes plural.

> *sons*-in-law

Irregular Plurals
An irregular plural is a noun that is made plural in any other way. Certain words do not change.

> deer, sheep and moose

Any noun ending in 'fe', change the 'f' to 'v' and add 's.'

> *knife* becomes *knives*

A noun ending in 'f', change the 'f' to 've' and add 's.'

> *wolf* becomes *wolves*

A noun ending in 'o', add an 'es' on the end.

> *potato* becomes *potatoes*

A noun ending in 'us', change the 'us' to 'i.'

> *cactus* becomes *cacti*

A noun ending with 'on', changes the 'on' to an 'a.'

> *phenomenon* becomes *phenomena*

All Kinds
If the noun includes all kinds in a group, you can change the vowel, the word or add a different ending.

> *man* becomes *men*
> *goose* becomes *geese*
> *mouse* becomes *mice*

Unchanging
There are some nouns that the singular and plural are the same.
We refer to *sheep* and *deer* in both the singular and plural with one word.

Odds and Ends

Pluralize specific letters by adding an apostrophe and an 's' to ensure you are clear on your meaning.

> Remember to dot your I's and cross your T's before sending the memo.
> How many i's are in Mississippi?

Pluralize proper names by adding 's' to the end of the name. However, if a proper name ends with an 's,' 'x,' 'ch,' or 'sh,' add 'es.'

> There are three Anns in the class.
> There are only two Jameses and two Ashes in the class.

Treat collective nouns (groups of people, animals, or things) as singular. To lay stress on the individual members, rather than on the overall unit, treat the noun as plural.

> The warren is home to a local herd of rabbits.
> A herd of rabbits are eating my crops.

Possessives

A possessive noun implies 'a' or 'of the' before it.

> The bone of the dog can be said The dog's bone.

A possessive can be singular or plural.

Singular Possessives

Add an 's' to the end of a noun to make it possessive.

> the girl's blue knapsack

Plural Possessives

Add an apostrophe ' to the end of a singular plural noun that ends in 's' to make it possessive.

> All the musicians' instruments were stolen.

Add an ''s' to a plural noun that ends in a letter other than 's' to make it possessive.

> The children's laughter was infectious.

Proper Names

Add "'s' to a proper name to make it possessive.

> Lilly's lipstick is a pretty shade of pink.

If a singular noun ends in 's,' either add an ' 's' to the end of the word or place the apostrophe ' " at the end of the word.

> Charles' book, James's car, Mr. Roberts' case, Achilles' tendon

Possessive Pronouns

Do not use an apostrophe to indicate possession for a possessive pronoun, or for the possessive form of it.

> Is that *your* car?
> No, *ours* is the dark blue one at the end.

It's vs Its

The rule is: if you can replace 'it's' with 'it is' or 'it has,' use 'it's.'

> It's one of a kind.
> This can also be written: It is one of a kind.

Otherwise, use 'its.'

> The dog lost its collar.

Who, Whom, Whoever, Whomever

Use the he/him method to decide which word is correct.

he = who
him = whom

> Who wrote the letter? (He wrote the letter.)
> For whom do I vote? (I vote for him.)

Who/Whom/Whoever/Whomever Exercise

Choose the correct word for each sentence.

1. _____ drank all the milk?
2. _____ are you referring to in this sentence?
3. _____ is your favourite hockey player?
4. The police have a good idea of _____ committed the crime.
5. He will talk about poetry with _____ asks him.

6. _____ left their lunch in the refrigerator, can you please remove it?
7. I asked _____ she was bringing to the party.
8. I wondered _____ John was currently dating.

Who vs. That vs. Which

For People and Things

The rule-of-thumb is: <u>who</u> refers to people; <u>that</u> and <u>which</u> refer to groups or things.

> Linda is the one who loves animals.
> Teddy belongs to the organization that supports people with disabilities.

Clauses

That introduces essential clauses, whereas *which* introduces non-essential clauses.

> I don't believe in *that* 'green product' label because anybody can call their product green.
> The organisation promoting healthier living, *which* usually only advertises electronically, created a billboard on a well-travelled part of the highway.

Remember: Essential clauses do not have commas surrounding them.

Commas surround nonessential clauses. These clauses can be removed and the sentence will still make sense.

Using **this, that, these,** or **those** to introduce an essential clause allows you to use which to introduce the next clause, whether it is essential or nonessential.

> That is a choice about which you should think very hard.

Writing Numbers

There are very specific rules when we write out numbers. For single digit numbers, you write out the number. Numbers higher than nine should be written in numerals. You need to be consistent with your numbering.

> Within the class, 10 students have dogs for pets and eight people have birds for pets. Of the 30 students taking three classes per day, we can schedule 10 students in one class and make it equal.

Spell out simple fractions and use hyphens with them. A mixed fraction can be expressed in figures unless it is the first word of a sentence.

Express large numbers in the simplest format. Round numbers are usually spelled out. Be careful to be consistent within a sentence.

> You can earn anywhere from one million dollars to five million dollars.

Write decimals in figures. Put a zero in front of a decimal unless the decimal itself begins with a zero.

If the number includes a decimal point, use a comma only when the number has five or more digits before the decimal point. Place the comma in front of the third digit to the left of the decimal point. Use the comma where it would appear in the figure format. Use the word and where the decimal point appears in the figure format.

> $25,500.50 – Twenty-five thousand, five hundred dollars and fifty cents.

When writing dates, use the appropriate abbreviation when the number precedes the month.

> June 30, 30th of June, April 1, 1st of April

Use numbers when referring to a specific year.

> 1995 was horrible for me.

Write decades out in full, using lowercase.

> During the nineties, a lot of companies closed shop.

If you are going to abbreviate them, include an apostrophe at the beginning.

> During the '80s, there was a lot of excess.

Normally, spell out the time of day in text even with half and quarter hours. With o'clock, the number is always spelled out.

> At five o'clock every day, I start dinner.

Use numerals with the time of day when exact times are being emphasized or when using A.M. or P.M.

> Classes start at 8:00 A.M. sharp.
> Instead of 12:00 P.M. and 12:00 A.M, you can use noon or midnight.

Numbers from twenty-one through ninety-nine should be hyphened.

> Forty-five dollars of your registration fee goes towards materials.

Do not use an apostrophes when pluralizing specific numbers.

> Programming code in binary is made up of 1s and 0s.

Write out a number if it begins a sentence.

> Forty-four people registered for the course. Only 22 arrived for the training session.

Common Style Mistakes

Word Choice

Tone

The tone of your communication is determined by your word choice. You will read different tones in scientific journals, academic journals, or even in different newspapers or magazines. The tone selected for a communication is determined by two factors: your audience and your purpose.

You need to know your audience and your purpose before you begin writing. Ask yourself (or whoever assigned you the writing task to you) the following questions:

> 1. Who is my audience? A general public with little knowledge of the topic? A technical audience? An audience who knows a lot about the topic already?

> 2. What is the purpose of the communication? To influence opinion? To describe a situation? To inform the audience of a particular problem and present a resolution?

Answering these questions will determine the level of detail and the words you choose, and therefore create the tone in your communication.

Misused Words Exercise

Circle the correct word.

1. They did not accept / except money for their work.
2. The heat had a bad health affect / effect on Troy.
3. She gave me some sound advise / advice.
4. It wasn't idea / ideal, but it got the job done.
5. Its / it's getting late.
6. They were lead / led to their table by the server.
7. People think Jimi Hendrix was a better guitar player than / then Jimmy Page.
8. I was to / too tired to /too go out last night, so I stayed in and watched Netflix.
9. She was already / all ready to go and then her son got sick.
10. Except / accept for Rodolfo, all of the workers were lazy.
11. The detective followed a lead / led to the culprit.
12. His deed weighed heavily on his conscious / conscience.

Active and Passive Voice
In most cases, you are going to write using the active voice. This means that the subject of the sentence is doing something. Passive voice has the subject of the sentence being acted upon.

> I broke the window. (Active voice)
> The window was broken by me. (Passive voice)

Although there are some circumstances when passive voice is acceptable, it is generally accepted that you use the active voice (or active verb pattern) as frequently as possible. "I" is the first person singular subject pronoun, referring to the person performing the action. "We" is the plural of two or more people performing an action.

> I jogged for two hours last night.
> We went to the movies last night.

Flow

Transitions
The "flow" in communications is how well you guide your audience from one thought to the next. Transitional words aid you in doing this in a communication.

Linking Words and Phrases

The following list of words can assist you in making smooth transitions between ideas and create a smooth flow in your document:

although	as a result	as a result of	because
because of	conversely	despite the fact	even though
for example	for instance	furthermore	hence
however	i.e.	in addition	in contrast
in fact	in other words	in spite of	moreover
nevertheless	on the contrary	on the other hand	that is
unlike			

Capitalization Rules

When to Use Capitals
- the first word of a quoted sentence
- proper nouns
- a title when it precedes a name
- a title when it follows the name on the address or signature line
- a title of a high-ranking government official (when it is used before their names)
- any title used as a direct address
- compass points when they refer to specific regions (for example: "Three relatives from the South arrived yesterday.")
- compass points referring to a street name/address
- the first and last words of titles of publications regardless of their parts of speech
- words within titles, including the short verb forms Is, Are, and Be
- federal or state when used as part of an official agency name or in government documents where these terms represent an official name
- department, bureau, and office if you have already set the term (for example: Canadian Wheat Bureau. The Bureau overseas….)
- the first word of a salutation and the first word of a complimentary close
- words derived from proper nouns
- specific course titles
- when two or more sentences follow a sentence ending with a colon

When Not to Use Capitals
- a civic title if it is used instead of the name
- a title that is acting as a description following the name
- words within titles such as a, an, the, but, as, if, and, or, nor, or prepositions
- federal or state when used as part of an official agency name or in government documents being used as general terms
- names of seasons
- the first word if it begins a list following a colon
- when only one sentence follows a sentence ending with a colon

Faulty Parallelism
Parallel sentences are sentences in which the elements appear in a list or series, in compound structures, in comparisons using that or as, and in contrasted elements, when two or more parts of the sentence are parallel in meaning and form. Most faulty parallel sentences occur when elements within the sentence do not agree.

> She prepared her essays slowly and with care. (faulty)
> She prepared her essays slowly and carefully. (correct)

> He enjoys riding his bike and to read novels. (faulty)
> He enjoys riding his bike and reading novels. (correct)

> I like to shop, travel and listening to music. (faulty)
> I like shopping, travelling and listening to music. (correct)
> I like to shop, travel and listen to music. (correct)

Dangling Modifiers
A dangling modifier is a word or phrase, usually at the start of a sentence that does not connect properly to the rest of the sentence, because it is placed so far away from what it is describing.

> Having been thrown across the room, the dog caught the bone. (dangling)
> The dog caught the bone thrown across the room. (correct)

Misplaced Modifiers
A misplaced modifier is a word or phrase incorrectly placed and appears to be describing the wrong thing.

> That student has nearly annoyed every professor she has had. (misplaced modifier)
> The student has annoyed nearly every professor she has had. (correct)